1983

CASE AND DOCUMENTARY SUPPLEMENT

For use with

BASIC

CORPORATION LAW

MATERIALS—CASES—TEXT

SECOND EDITION

Edited by

DETLEV F. VAGTS

Professor of Law, Harvard University

Mineola, New York
THE FOUNDATION PRESS, INC.
1983

Vagts Basic Corp.Law 2nd Ed. UCB
1983 Supp.

PREFACE

This Case and Documentary Supplement is for use in connection with the second edition of my book, Basic Corporation Law. Part A contains documentary materials. Some of the materials are statutes, federal and state, or analogous bodies of law: regulations, Restatements, etc. Note that I have not included the Delaware General Corporation Law or other statute. I assume that you will obtain a separate pamphlet issued by the Secretary of State of Delaware containing an up-to-date version, or, if the course as taught focuses on the law of some other state, a corresponding pamphlet. Other documents are private handiwork and are included simply as models. Of particular importance are the articles of incorporation and the by-laws. These are the constitutive documents upon which a corporation is constructed. A student should become used to relating the two documents to each other and to the governing corporation law. Both were drafted by experienced craftsmen and both are for a corporation organized in Delaware. Note, however, that they were not drafted by the same person or at the same time; the by-laws are considerably older. In fact there are instructive discrepancies between the by-laws and the Delaware corporation law in its present form; the student should be alert for these. There will inevitably be other discrepancies between those documents and the laws of any other jurisdiction.

Part B includes a limited number of important recent decisions of the United States and Delaware courts. Contrary to the practice in the casebook itself, the numbers of those footnotes that have been kept in the editing correspond to their numbers in the original text and have not been renumbered sequentially.

Statutes and rules were checked for currency through the end of 1982.

The following courtesies ought to be, and hereby are, acknowledged. The American Law Institute permitted me to reprint the Certificate of Incorporation and the Restatement (Second) of Agency excerpts. The National Conference of Commissioners on Uniform State Law gave permission with respect to the Uniform Acts excerpted herein. General Dynamics Corporation, through its Secretary, John Maguire, permitted reproduction of its stock certificate form; this was arranged by Mr. Keeley of Columbian Security Banknote with the *nil obstat* of the New York Stock Exchange.

DETLEV F. VAGTS

Cambridge, Massachusetts
May, 1983

TABLE OF CONTENTS

A. LAWS AND DOCUMENTS

Part I.   Corporate Documents

Part II.   Federal Statutes and Regulations

Part III.   State Statutes and Regulations

B.   RECENT CASES

*

Case and Documentary Supplement

FOR USE WITH
MATERIALS—CASES—TEXT
ON
BASIC CORPORATION LAW

A. LAWS AND DOCUMENTS

Part I
CORPORATE DOCUMENTS

A. SAMPLE CERTIFICATE OF INCORPORATION

[The following sample certificate of incorporation has been reprinted from George Seward's Basic Corporate Practice. Copyright 1966. Reprinted with the permission of the American Law Institute. The certificate has been amended to reflect changes suggested by the author in a 1969 Supplement to Basic Corporate Practice, the Supplement being copyrighted by The American Law Institute in 1969. It should be noted that on page 14 of the 1969 Supplement the author notes that an alternate form of Certificate of Incorporation is suggested, the text being set out in the Supplement in light of the 1967 revision of the Delaware General Corporation Law[1] While the author states it is not necessarily a substitute for the form reproduced herein, the new material is more concise and for most situations probably preferable. The original has footnotes which key the text to the Delaware statutes and other authorities. For the sake of realism and simplicity these have been omitted.]

CERTIFICATE OF INCORPORATION

OF

DELAWARE EXAMPLE CORPORATION

FIRST. The name of the corporation is DELAWARE EXAMPLE CORPORATION.

[1] A like form appears in the second edition, 1977, by Seward & Nauss.

SECOND. The principal office of the corporation in the State of Delaware is to be located at No._____ Street, Wilmington, New Castle County. Its resident agent at such address is (name).

THIRD. The nature of the business of the corporation and its objects are:

     A. (Insert a general description of the proposed business such as "To transact the textile business and all other business not forbidden by law;");

     B. To manufacture, buy, sell and deal in goods, wares, merchandise and personal property of every kind;

     C. To the same extent as natural persons could do, to acquire, construct, maintain, develop, improve, rent, use, mortgage and dispose of real property and interests,

     D. To act as agent or representative, in any capacity; and to perform services for others;

     E. To acquire, develop, improve, use, grant licenses in respect of, mortgage, dispose of and deal in letters patent of the United States and of any foreign country, patent rights, licenses and privileges, inventions, improvements and processes, copyrights, trademarks and trade names;

     F. To acquire, own and dispose of rights, privileges, permits and franchises convenient for any of the purposes of its business;

     G. To acquire, own, pledge, dispose of and deal in shares of capital stock, rights, bonds, debentures, notes, trust receipts and other securities, obligations, choses in action and evidences of indebtedness or interest issued or created by any corporations, associations, firms, trusts or persons, public or private, or by the government of the United States of America, or by any foreign government or by any state, territory, province, municipality or other political subdivision or by any governmental agency, domestic or foreign, and as owner thereof to possess and exercise all the rights, powers and privileges of ownership, including the right to execute consents and vote thereon and to do any and all acts and things necessary or advisable for the preservation, protection, improvement and enhancement in value thereof;

     H. To aid in any manner any corporation, association, firm or individual, any of whose securities, evidences of indebtedness, obligations or stock are held by the corporation directly or indirectly, or in which, or in the welfare of which, the corporation shall have any interest, and to guarantee securities, evidences of indebtedness and obligations of other persons, firms, associations and corporations;

I.   To acquire, and pay for in cash, stock, bonds or other securities of the corporation or otherwise, the goodwill, rights, assets and property and to undertake and assume the whole or any part of the obligations or liabilities of any person, firm, association or corporation;

J.   To enter into, make and perform contracts of every kind;

K.   To borrow moneys and, from time to time without limit as to amount, to issue, accept, endorse and execute promissory notes, drafts, bills of exchange, warrants, bonds, debentures and other negotiable or non-negotiable instruments and evidences of indebtedness, and to secure the payment of any thereof and of the interest thereon by mortgage upon or pledge, conveyance or assignment in trust of the whole or any part of the property of the corporation, whether at the time owned or thereafter acquired, and to sell, pledge or otherwise dispose of such bonds or other obligations of the corporation for its corporate purposes;

L.   To lend any of its funds, either with or without security;

M.   To acquire, hold and dispose of shares of its own capital stock and rights thereto;

N.   To carry on any other lawful business for which a corporation may be organized under the General Corporation Law of Delaware;

O.   To carry out all or any part of the foregoing purposes as principal or agent, or in conjunction with any other person, firm, association or corporation, or as a partner or member of a partnership, syndicate or joint venture or otherwise, and in any part of the world to the same extent and as fully as natural persons might or could do;

P.   To do all such things as are necessary and incidental to the attainment of the above stated purposes;

Q.   To have and exercise all the powers conferred by the laws of the State of Delaware upon corporations formed under the laws of such State;

R. The purposes specified in the foregoing clauses shall, except as otherwise expressed, be in nowise limited or restricted by reference to, or inference from, the terms of any other clause in this certificate of incorporation, but the purposes specified in each of the foregoing clauses of this article shall be regarded as independent purposes.

The above stated objects and purposes shall be construed also as powers, but such enumeration of specific powers shall not be held to limit or restrict in any manner the powers of the corporation now or hereafter granted to it by law. Only the business for which a corporation may be formed under the laws of the State of Delaware may be concucted by the corporation.

FOURTH (<u>providing transfer restrictions and a purchase option in the corporation and the stockholders</u>). The total number of shares of stock which the corporation shall have authority to issue is ten thousand and the par value of such shares is one dollar, amounting in the aggregate to ten thousand dollars. Shares shall not be transferable to any purchaser thereof unless such shares shall first have been offered for sale to the corporation and, if such shares shall not have been purchased by the corporation, such shares shall have been offered for sale to the stockholders of the corporation, all in accordance with provisions to be stated in the by-laws.

ALTERNATIVE FOURTH (<u>providing for two classes of common stock, one non-voting and one voting</u>). The total number of shares of stock which the corporation shall have authority to issue is one thousand, all of which shall be without par value. Five hundred of such shares shall be Class A voting shares and five hundred shall be Class B non-voting shares. The Class A shares and the Class B shares shall have identical rights, without regard to class except that the Class B shares shall not entitle the holder thereof to vote on any matter unless specifically required by law.

SECOND ALTERNATIVE FOURTH (<u>providing for preferred stock</u>). The total number of shares of all classes of stock which the corporation shall have authority to issue is one thousand of which one hundred shares of the par value of one hundred dollars each, amounting in the aggregate to ten thousand dollars, shall be preferred stock and nine hundred shares of the par value of one dollar each, amounting in the aggregate to nine hundred dollars, shall be common stock.

The designations and the powers, preferences and rights, and the qualifications, limitations or restrictions thereof of the classes of stock of the corporation are as follows:

The preferred stock shall be designated "5% Cumulative Preferred Stock" (hereinafter called the "Preferred Stock") and the common stock shall be designated "Common Stock."

The holders of the Preferred Stock shall be entitled to receive, when and as declared by the board of directors out of funds legally available therefor, cumulative preferential dividends in cash at the rate of, but not exceeding, 5% of the par value per annum, payable quarterly on the first days of March, June, September and December in each year. Dividends on the first issue of shares of Preferred Stock shall commence to accrue and be cumulative, whether or not declared, from and after the date of issue thereof. Dividends on shares of Preferred Stock subsequently issued shall commence to accrue and be cumulative, whether or not declared, from and after the date which will make the rights of the holders of such subsequently issued shares in respect of unpaid dividends the same as the rights of the holders of the then outstanding shares. So long as any of the Preferred Stock remains outstanding, in no event shall any dividend whatever be paid upon or declared or set apart for the Common Stock, nor shall any Common Stock be purchased, retired or otherwise acquired by the corporation, unless and until all dividends on the then outstanding shares of Preferred Stock for all past quarterly dividend periods shall have been paid or declared and set apart for payment, but without interest, and the full dividends thereon for the then current quarterly dividend period shall have been concurrently paid or declared and set apart for payment. After such full dividends on the Preferred Stock shall have been so paid or declared and set apart for payment, then and not otherwise dividends may be declared and paid on the Common Stock when and as determined by the board of directors out of any funds legally available for dividends.

The corporation at the option of the board of directors may at any time or from time to time redeem all or any part of the Preferred Stock then outstanding upon notice duly given as hereinafter provided, by paying therefor in cash the sum of one hundred dollars per share plus an amount in cash equal to the accrued and unpaid dividends thereon to the date fixed for redemption. In case less than all of the outstanding shares of Preferred Stock are to be redeemed, the shares to be redeemed shall be selected pro rata or by lot or by such other equitable method as the board of directors may determine. Notice of redemption of any shares of Preferred Stock shall be mailed, postage pre-paid, to the holders of record of the shares to be redeemed at their respective addresses then appearing on the books of the corporation, not less than fifteen nor more than sixty days prior to the date designated for such redemption. If such notice of redemption shall have been duly given, and if on or before the redemption date named therein the funds necessary for such redemption shall have been set aside by the corporation in trust for the account of the holders of the Preferred Stock so called for redemption so as to be and continue available therefor, then, from and after the giving of such notice and the setting aside of such funds, notwithstanding that any certificate for shares of Preferred Stock so called for redemption shall not have been surrendered for cancellation, the shares represented thereby shall no longer be deemed outstanding, and the holders of such certificate or certificates shall have with respect to such stock no rights in or with respect to the corporation except the right to receive the redemption price thereof and an amount in cash equal to accrued and unpaid dividends thereon to the date designated for redemption, without interest, upon the surrender of such certificate or certificates. The term "an amount in cash equal to accrued and unpaid dividends" with respect to any share of Preferred Stock shall mean an amount computed at the rate of 5% per annum on the par value of such share for the period from the date upon which dividends thereon commenced to accrue and be cumulative to the date as of which accrued and unpaid dividends are being determined, less the amount of all dividends theretofore paid on such share.

In the event of any voluntary or involuntary liquidation, dissolution or winding up of the affairs of the corporation, the holders of the Preferred Stock shall be entitled to receive one hundred dollars in cash for each share thereof, together with an amount in cash equal to accrued and unpaid dividends thereon to the date of such payment, before any distribution of the assets of the corporation shall be made to the holders of Common Stock. After such payment shall have been

made in full to the holders of the outstanding
Preferred Stock or funds necessary for such payment shall have been set aside in trust for the
account of the holders of the outstanding Preferred Stock so as to be and continue available
therefor, the holders of the outstanding Preferred
Stock shall be entitled to no further participation
in such distribution of the assets of the corporation,
and the remaining assets of the corporation shall
be divided and distributed among
the holders of the Common Stock then outstanding
according to their respective shares. If, upon
such liquidation, dissolution or winding up, the
assets of the corporation distributable as aforesaid among the holders of the Preferred Stock shall
be insufficient to permit the payment to them of
said amount, the entire assets shall be distributed
ratably among the holders of the Preferred Stock.
A consolidation or merger of the corporation, a sale
or transfer of all or substantially all of its
assets as an entirety, or any purchase or redemption of stock of the corporation of any class,
shall not be regarded as a "liquidation, dissolution
or winding up of the affairs of the corporation"
within the meaning of this paragraph.

If on the date fixed by the by-laws for the
holding of the annual meeting of stockholders any
dividend accrued on the Preferred Stock for any
past quarterly dividend period shall not have been
declared and paid, then at such annual meeting the
holders of Preferred Stock voting as a separate
class shall be entitled to elect a majority of the
directors of the corporation and the balance of the
directors shall be elected by the holders of the
Common Stock voting as a separate class. Directors so elected shall hold office until the
next annual meeting of stockholders and until
the election of their successors.

Except as expressly required by law and as
herein provided, the holders of the Preferred Stock
shall have no voting power nor shall they be entitled to notice of meetings of stockholders, all
rights to vote and all voting power being vested
exclusively in the holders of the Common Stock.

No holder of stock of the corporation shall
be entitled as a metter of right, preemptive or
otherwise, to subscribe for or purchase any part of
any stock now or hereafter authorized to be issued,
or shares thereof held in the treasury of the corporation or securities convertible into stock,
whether issued for cash or other consideration or
by way of dividend or otherwise.

THIRD ALTERNATIVE FOURTH (providing for preferred stock to be issued in series). The total number of shares of all classes of stock which the corporation shall have authority to issue is one thousand of which one hundred shares of the par value of one hundred dollars each, amounting in the aggregate to ten thousand dollars, shall be preferred stock and nine hundred shares of the par value of one dollar each, amounting in the aggregate to nine hundred dollars, shall be common stock.

The preferred stock may be issued from time to time in one or more series. The designations, preferences and other rights and limitations or restrictions of the preferred stock of each series shall be such as are stated and expressed herein, shall be such as may be fixed by the board of directors (authority so to do being hereby expressly granted) and stated and expressed in a resolution or resolutions adopted by the board of directors providing for the initial issue of preferred stock of such series. Such resolution or resolutions shall (a) fix the dividend rights of holders of shares of such series, (b) fix the terms on which stock of such series may be redeemed if the shares of such series are to be redeemable, (c) fix the rights of the holders of stock of such series upon dissolution or any distribution of assets, (d) fix the terms or amount of the sinking fund, if any, to be provided for the purchase or redemption of stock of such series, (e) fix the terms upon which the stock of such series may be converted into or exchanged for stock of any other class or classes or of any one or more series of preferred stock if the shares of such series are to be convertible or exchangeable, (f) fix the voting rights, if any, of the shares of such series and (g) fix such other designations, preferences and relative, participating, optional or other special rights, and qualifications, limitations or restrictions thereof desired to be so fixed.

Except to the extent otherwise provided in the resolution or resolutions of the board of directors providing for the initial issue of shares of a particular series or expressly required by law, holders of shares of preferred stock of any series shall be entitled to one vote for each share thereof so held, shall vote share for share with the holders of the common stock without distinction as to class and shall not be entitled to vote separately as a class or series of a class. The number of shares of preferred stock may be increased or decreased from time to time by the affirmative vote of the holders of a majority of the stock of the corporation entitled to vote, and the holders of the preferred stock shall not be entitled to vote separately as a class or series of a class on any such increase or decrease.

All shares of any one series of preferred stock shall be identical with each other in all respects except that shares of any one series issued at different times may differ as to the dates from which dividends thereon shall accumulate, and all series of preferred stock shall rank equally and be identical in all respects except as specified in the respective resolutions of the board of directors providing for the initial issue thereof.

Subject to the prior and superior rights of the preferred stock as set forth in any resolution or resolutions of the board of directors providing for the initial issue of a particular series of preferred stock, such dividends (payable in cash, stock or otherwise) as may be determined by the board of directors may be declared and paid on the common stock from time to time out of any funds legally available therefor and the preferred stock shall not be entitled to participate in any such dividend.

No holder of stock of the corporation shall be entitled as a matter of right, preemptive or otherwise, to subscribe for or purchase any part of any stock now or hereafter authorized to be issued, or shares thereof held in the treasury of the corporation or securities convertible into stock, whether issued for cash or other consideration or by way of dividend or otherwise.

FIFTH. The minimum amount of capital with which the corporation will commence business is one thousand dollars.

SIXTH. The name and mailing address of the incorporator is:

****

****

NINTH. In furtherance and not in limitation of the powers conferred by statute, the board of directors is expressly authorized.

A. Subject to by-laws adopted by the stockholders, to make, alter or repeal the by-laws of the corporation;

B. To authorize and cause to be executed mortgages and liens, with or without limit as to amount, upon the real and personal property of the corporation;

C. To authorize the guaranty by the corporation of securities, evidences of indebtedness and obligations of other persons, corporations and business entities;

D. To set apart out of any of the funds of the corporation available for dividends a reserve or reserves for any proper purpose and to abolish any such reserve;

E. By resolution adopted by a majority of the whole board, to designate one or more committees, each committee to consist of two or more of the directors of the corporation, which, to the extent provided in the resolution or in the by-laws of the corporation, shall have and may exercise the powers of the board of directors in the management of the business and affairs of the corporation, and may authorize the seal of the corporation to be affixed to all papers which, may require it. Such committee or committees shall have such name or names as may be stated in the by-laws of the corporation or as may be determined from time to time by resolution adopted by the board of directors.

All corporate powers of the corporation shall be exercised by the board of directors except as otherwise provided herein or by law.

TENTH. Any property of the corporation less than all of its assets including goodwill and its corporate franchise, deemed by the board of directors to be not essential to the conduct of the business of the corporation, may be sold, leased, exchanged or otherwise disposed of by authority of the board of directors. All of the property and assets of the corporation including its goodwill and its corporate franchises, may be sold, leased or exchanged upon such terms and conditions and for such consideration (which may be in whole or in part shares of stock and/or other securities of any other corporation or corporations and/or money or other property) as the board of directors shall deem expedient and for the best interests of the corporation, when and as authorized by the affirmative vote of the holders of a majority of the stock issued and outstanding having voting power given at a stockholders' meeting duly called for that purpose, or when authorized by the written consent of the holders of a majority of the voting stock issued and outstanding.

ELEVENTH. A director or officer of the corporation shall not be disqualified by his office from dealing or contracting with the corporation either as a vendor, purchaser or otherwise, nor shall any transaction or contract of the corporation be void or voidable by reason of the fact that any director or officer or any firm of which any director or officer is a member or any corporation of which any director or officer is a stockholder, officer or director, is in any way interested in such transaction or contract, provided that such transaction or contract is or shall be authorized, ratified or approved either (1) by a vote of a majority of a quorum of the board of directors or of an executive committee thereof, without counting in such majority any director so interested (although any director so interested may be included in such quorum), or (2) by a majority of a quorum of the stockholders entitled to vote at any meeting. No director or officer shall be liable to account to the corporation for any profits realized from any such transaction or contract authorized, ratified or approved as aforesaid by reason of the fact that he, or any firm of which he is a member or any corporation of which he is a stockholder, officer or director was interested in such transaction or contract. Nothing herein contained shall create liability in the events above described or prevent the authorization, ratification or approval of such contracts in any other manner permitted by law.

TWELFTH. No person shall be liable to the corporation for any loss or damage suffered by it on account of any action taken or omitted to be taken by him as a director or officer of the corporation in good faith, if such person (i) exercised or used the same degree of diligence, care and skill as an ordinarily prudent man would have exercised or used under the circumstances in the conduct of his own affairs, or (ii) took, or omitted to take, such action in reliance upon advice of counsel for the corporation, or upon statements made or information furnished by officers or employees of the corporation which he had reasonable grounds to believe to be true, or upon a financial statement of the corporation prepared by an officer or employee of the corporation in charge of its accounts or certified by a public accountant or firm of public accountants.

THIRTEENTH. Any contract, transaction or act of the corporation or of the board of directors which shall be approved or ratified by a majority of a quorum of the stockholders entitled to vote at any meeting shall be as valid and binding as though approved or ratified by every stockholder of the corporation; but any failure of the stockholders to approve or ratify such contract, transaction or act, when and if submitted, shall not be deemed in any way to invalidate the same or to deprive the corporation, its directors or officers of their right to proceed with such contract, transaction or act.

FOURTEENTH. Every person who was or is a party or is threatened to be made a party to or is involved in any action, suit or proceeding, whether civil, criminal, administrative or investigative, by reason of the fact that he or a person of whom he is the legal representative is or was a director or officer of the corporation or is or was serving at the request of the corporation as a director of officer of another corporation, or as its representative in a partnership, joint venture, trust or other enterprise, shall be indemnified and held harmless to the fullest extent legally permissible under the General Corporation Law of the State of Delaware from time to time against all expenses, liability and loss (including attorneys' fees, judgments, fines and amounts paid or to be paid in settlement) reasonably incurred or suffered by him in connection therewith. Such right of indemnification shall be a contract right which may be enforced in any manner desired by such person. Such right of indemnification shall not be exclusive of any other right which such directors, officers, or representatives may have or hereafter acquire and, without limiting the generality of such statement, they shall be entitled to their respective rights of indemnification under any by-law, agreement, vote of stockholders, provision of law or otherwise, as well as their rights under this Article.

The board of directors may adopt by-laws from time to time with respect to indemnification to provide at all times the fullest indemnification permitted by the General Corporation Law of the State of Delaware and may cause the corporation to purchase and maintain insurance on behalf of any person who is or was a director or officer of the corporation, or is or was serving at the request of the corporation as a director or officer of another corporation, or as its representative in a partnership, joint venture, trust or other enterprise against any liability asserted against such person and incurred in any such capacity or arising out of such status, whether or not the corporation would have the power to indemnify such person.

FIFTEENTH: Whenever a compromise or arrangement is proposed between this corporation and its creditors or any class of them and/or between this corporation and its stockholders or any class of them, any court of equitable jurisdiction within the State of Delaware may, on the application in a summary way of this corporation or of any creditor or stockholder thereof, or on the application of any receiver or receivers appointed for this corporation under the provisions of section 291 of Title 8 of the Delaware Code or on the application of trustees in dissolution or of any receiver or receivers appointed for this corporation under the provisions of section 279 of Title 8 of the Delaware Code order a meeting of the creditors or class of creditors, and/or of the stockholders or class of stockholders of this corporation, as the case may be, to be summoned in such manner as the said court directs. If a majority in number represent-

ing three-fourths in value of the creditors or class of
creditors, and/or of the stockholders or class of stockholders of this corporation, as the case may be, agree to
any compromise or arrangement and to any reorganization of
this corporation as consequence of such compromise or arrangement, the said compromise or arrangement and the said reorganization shall, if sanctioned by the court to which the said
application has been made, be binding on all the creditors
or class of creditors, and/or on all the stockholders or
class of stockholders, of this corporation, as the case
may be, and also on this corporation.

SIXTEENTH.   Meetings of stockholders and directors may
be held outside the State of Delaware, if the by-laws so
provide.   The books of account of the corporation may be
kept outside the State of Delaware at such place or places
as may be designated from time to time by the board
of directors or in the by-laws of the corporation.   Elections of directors need not be by ballot unless the by-
laws of the corporation shall so provide.

SEVENTEENTH.   The corporation reserves the right to
amend, alter, change or repeal any provision contained in
this certificate of incorporation, in the manner now or
hereafter prescribed by statute, and all rights conferred
upon stockholders herein are granted subject to this
reservation.

EIGHTEENTH.   Whenever a vote of stockholders at a meeting thereof is required or permitted to be taken in connection with any corporate action, the meeting and vote may be
dispensed with if such number of stockholders who, if voting,
could have authorized such action shall consent in writing to
such corporate action being taken.   Prompt notice shall be
given by the secretary to all stockholders of the taking of
corporate action without a meeting by less than unanimous
written consent; but the failure of the secretary to give
such notice shall not affect the validity of such corporate
action.

IN WITNESS WHEREOF the undersigned, for the purpose of
forming a corporation pursuant to the General Corporation
Law of the State of Delaware, do make this certificate September 15, 1965.

_____ (Seal)

_____ (Seal)

_____ (Seal)

STATE OF   )
) ss.:
COUNTY OF   )

BE IT REMEMBERED that on September 15, 1965, personally come before me, a Notary Public for the State
of   all of the parties to the foregoing certificate of incorporation, known to me personally to be
such, and severally acknowledged the said certificate
to be the act and deed of the signers respectively and
that the facts therein stated are truly set forth.

GIVEN under my hand and seal of office the day
and year aforesaid.

_____
                                Notary Public

B. SAMPLE BY-LAWS

WARNING: These by-laws are to be used for classroom use only.
Do not assume that you can use them in practice, except
after thinking through your needs and personally mastering
the contents. Every corporate lawyer has his own ideas about
by-laws (and is dissatisfied with everybody else's). No
warranty is made that these by-laws fit comfortably with the
present Delaware Corporation Law or with the sample Certificate of Incorporation. In fact, they were drafted some
years ago and do not reflect recent changes.

BY-LAWS OF XYZ COMPANY

Article I

OFFICES

The principal office of the corporation in the State
of Delaware shall be in the City of Dover, County of Kent,
and the name of the resident agent in charge is Sweden
Trust Company, 110 South Street, Dover, Delaware.

The corporation shall also have offices at such other
places without as well as within the State of Delaware,
as the Board of Directors may from time to time determine.

Article II

STOCKHOLDERS

Place of Meeting

SECTION 1-- All meetings of the stockholders for the
election of directors shall be held at the office of the
corporation in the City of Cambridge, State of Massachusetts. Meetings of stockholders for any other purpose may
be held at such place, within or without the State of Delaware, as may be stated in the notice of meeting or in a
duly executed waiver thereof.

Annual Meeting

SECTION 2-- The Annual Meeting of Stockholders shall
be held the second Friday in April each year, unless said day
be a legal holiday, in which case the Annual Meeting shall be held
on the next day thereafter not a legal holiday, for the purpose
of electing directors and for the transaction of such other business as may be brought before the meeting.

Special Meetings

SECTION 3 -- A special meeting of the stockholders may be
called at any time by the Board of Directors, and shall
be called   by the Board of Directors upon the written request of
the holder or holders of records of shares amounting to one-fourth
or more of the capital stock of the corporation then issued and
outstanding and entitled to vote at such meeting. In calling any
special meeting the Board of Directors shall specify in the call
the object and place of the meeting, and no new matter not so specified shall be introduced or considered at such meeting or any
adjournment thereof.

Notice of Meeting

SECTION 4-- Written notice of the day, place and hour of each
Annual Meeting, and the day, place, hour and purpose of each special meeting, shall be given to the holders of record of the shares
of stock of the corporation entitled to vote by mailing postage
prepaid or delivering in person such notice to each such holder
at his address appearing on the stock book of the corporation at
least ten days prior to such meeting. Failure to give notice of
any Annual Meeting, or any irregularity in such notice, shall not
affect the validity of any Annual Meeting or of any proceedings
at such meeting. The time and place of holding a meeting for the
election of directors shall not be changed within sixty days next
before the day on which the election is to be held and a notice

of any such change shall be given to each stockholder at least
twenty days before the election is held, in person or by letter
mailed to his last known post office address.

Quorum

SECTION 5-- At all meetings of the stockholders there shall
be present either in person or by proxy stockholders owning a majority of the shares outstanding and entitled to vote in order to
constitute a quorum. Except as otherwise provided by statute or
by the Certificate of Incorporation or the By-Laws of the corporation, the vote of a majority of any quorum shall be sufficient to
elect directors and to pass any resolution within the power of the
holders of all the outstanding shares.

If at any annual or special meeting of the stockholders a
quorum of stockholders shall not be present, a majority of those
present, without notice other than announcement at the meeting, may
adjourn the meeting from time to time until a quorum shall attend,
whereupon any business may be transacted at the meeting as though
held when originally convened. The Secretary of the corporation,
or in his absence an Assistant Secretary or an appointee of the
presiding officer of the meeting, shall act as the secretary of
the meeting.

Voting

SECTION 6-- At each meeting of the stockholders every
stockholder of the corporation shall be entitled to one vote
in person or by proxy for each share of stock having voting
power, in respect of the matter on which the vote is to be
taken, standing in his name on the books of the corporation
at the time of the closing of the transfer books for the meeting, or, if the books be not closed for any meeting, on the
record date fixed as provided in Section 5 of Article V of
these By-Laws for determining the stockholders entitled to
vote at such meeting, or, if the books be not closed and no
record date be fixed, at the time of the meeting; but, except where the transfer books of the corporation shall have
been closed or a date shall have been fixed as a record date
for the determination of stockholders entitled to vote as
provided in Section 5 of Article V hereof, no share of stock
shall be voted on at any election of directors which shall
have been transferred on the books of the corporation within
twenty days next preceding such election.

At least ten days before every election, a complete list
of stockholders entitled to vote at said election arranged
in alphabetical order, shall be lodged and open to the examination of any stockholder, for said period of ten days,
at the place where said election is to be held, and shall
be produced and kept at the time and place of election
during the whole time thereof and subject to the inspection
of any stockholder who may be present.

Whenever the vote of stockholders at a meeting thereof is required or permitted to be taken in connection with corporate action by any provision of the statutes or of the Certificate of Incorporation of the By-Laws of the corporation, the meeting and vote of stockholders may be dispensed with, if all of the stockholders who would have been entitled to vote upon the action if such meeting were held, shall consent in writing to such corporate action being taken.

Proxies

SECTION 7-- Any stockholder entitled to vote upon any matter at any meeting of stockholders may so vote by proxy; but no proxy shall be voted on after three years from its date, unless said proxy provides for a longer period for which it shall remain in force. Every proxy shall be in writing, subscribed by the stockholder or his duly authorized attorney, and shall be dated, but need not be sealed, witnessed or acknowledged. Proxies shall be delivered to the Secretary of the corporation before such meeting.

Article III

BOARD OF DIRECTORS

Number; Method of Election; Terms of Office and

Qualification

SECTION 1 -- The business, property and affairs of the corporation shall be managed and controlled by the Board of Directors. The number of directors shall be seven and, from time to time, by the vote of not less than a majority of the directors then in office, the Board of Directors may increase or decrease the number of directors.

The directors shall be elected at the Annual Meeting of stockholders, each to hold office for the term of one year and until his successor shall have been duly chosen and shall have qualified. Directors need not be stockholders. Any director may resign his office at any time by delivering his resignation in writing to the corporation, a nd the acceptance of such resignation unless required by the terms thereof shall not be necessary to make such resignation effective. Any and all vacancies in the Board of Directors, caused by death, resignation, removal, increase in the number of directors, or otherwise, may be filled by the vote of a majority of the remaining directors though less than a quorum.

If, for any reason, the Annual Meeting of stockholders for the election of directors shall not be held at the time appointed by these By-Laws, the directors shall cause the election to be held as soon thereafter as conveniently may be, and the directors then in office shall continue until such election shall have been held and their successors duly chosen and qualified.

Meetings

SECTION 2 -- The Board of Directors may hold its meetings and have an office and keep the books of the corporation, except as otherwise provided by the statutes of Delaware, in such place or places within or without the State of Delaware as the Board by resolution from time to time may determine.

The Board of Directors may in its discretion provide for regular or stated meetings of the Board. Notice of regular or stated meetings need not be given. Special meetings of the Board shall be held whenever called by direction of the President or any two of the directors for the time being in office. The Secretary shall give notice of such special meeting by mailing at least three days, or by telegraphing or telephoning the same at least one day, before the meeting to each director; but such notice may be waived by any director. Unless otherwise indicated in the notice thereof, any and all business may be transacted at a special meeting.

At any meeting at which every director shall be present, even though without notice, any business may be transacted. No notice of any adjourned meeting need be given.

The Board of Directors shall meet immediately after election, following the Annual Meeting of stockholders, for the purpose of organizing, for the election of corporate officers as hereinafter specified, and for the transaction of any other business which may come before it. No notice of such meeting shall be necessary.

Quorum

SECTION 3 -- Three directors shall constitute a quorum for the transaction of business; but if there shall be less than a quorum at any meeting of the Board a majority of those present may adjourn the meeting from time to time.

Compensation of Board of Directors

SECTION 4 -- Directors, as such, shall not receive any stated compensation for their services, but by resolution of the Board of Directors, a fixed sum and expenses of attendance, if any, may be allowed for attendance at each regular or special meeting thereof. Nothing in this Section shall be construed to preclude a director from serving the corporation in any other capacity and receiving compensation therefor.

Executive Committee

SECTION 5 -- The Board of Directors may in its discretion appoint an Executive Committee of three members. One of such members shall be elected Chairman of such Committee by the Board. The Executive Committee shall, between the meetings of the Board and while the Board is not in session, have all the powers and exercise all the duties of the Board of Directors in the management of the business of the corporation and shall report all action taken by it to the next succeeding meeting of the Board. Such action shall be subject to review by the Board, provided that no rights of third parties shall be affected by such review.

Meetings of the Executive Committee shall be called by the Secretary of the corporation from time to time at the direction and upon the request of the Chairman or any two members of the Executive Committee. Notice of such meetings shall in each instance be given to each member of the Committee at his last known business address at least one day before the meeting, either orally or in writing, delivered personally or by mail, or by telegraph or telephone.

Two members of the Executive Committee shall constitute a quorum for the transaction of business.

Article IV

OFFICERS

General Provisions

SECTION 1 -- The corporate officers of the corporation shall consist of a President (who shall be chosen from the Board of Directors), one or more

Vice Presidents, a Secretary, one or more Assistant Secretaries, a Treasurer, one or more Assistant Treasurers and such other officers as the Board of Directors may from time to time appoint. In so far as permitted by law, any two offices may be held by the same person. The foregoing officers, except those referred to in Section 2 of this Article IV, shall be elected by the Board of Directors at the first meeting after the stockholders' Annual Meeting in each year. They shall hold office, respectively, for the term of one year and until their respective successors shall have been chosen and shall have qualified.

Any officer elected or appointed by the Board of Directors may be removed at any time, with or without cause, by the affirmative vote of a majority of the whole Board of Directors.

Powers and Duties of the President

SECTION 2 -- The President shall preside at all meetings of the stockholders and of the Board of Directors and shall be the executive and administrative officer of the corporation. He shall have the power to appoint such officers, other than those whose election is provided for in the By-Laws, and also such agents and employees as in his judgment may be necessary or proper for the transaction of the business of the corporation, which powers shall include the appointment of such divisional or administrative Vice Presidents and such Assistant Secretaries and Assistant Treasurers as the President may from time to time deem necessary or appropriate, and shall determine their duties and fix their compensation, all subject to the ratification of the Board of Directors. He shall submit to the Board of Directors prior to the date of the Annual Meeting of stockholders, an annual report of the operations of the corporation during the preceding fiscal year, complete detailed statements of all income and expenditures, and a balance sheet showing the financial condition of the Corporation at the close of such fiscal year.

Powers and Duties of the Vice President

SECTION 3 -- The Vice Presidents shall
have such powers and perform such duties as
may from time to time be assigned to them
by the Board of Directors or the President.

Powers and Duties of the Secretary

SECTION 4 -- The Secretary or an Assistant Secretary
shall record the proceedings of all meetings of the Board
of Directors and the stockholders, in books kept for that
purpose. The Secretary shall be the custodian of the corporate seal, and he or an Assistant Secretary shall affix
the same to andcountersign papers requiring such acts; but
only on the order of the Board of Directors, the President
or a Vice President; and he and the Assistant Secretaries
shall perform such other duties as the Board, the President
or a designated Vice President shall assign to them.

Powers and Duties of the Treasurer

SECTION 5 -- The Treasurer and Assistant Treasurers
shall have care and custody of all funds and securities of
the corporation and disburse and administer the same under
the direction of the Board of Directors, the President or
designated Vice President; and shall perform such other duties
as the Board, the President or a designated Vice President
shall assign to them.

Salaries and Appointments

SECTION 6 -- The salaries of corporate officers shall
be fixed by the Board of Directors. The salaries of officers
not elected or appointed by the Board of Directors shall be
fixed by the President, subject to the approval of the Board.

Article V

CAPITAL STOCK

Certificates of Stock

SECTION 1 -- Certificates of stock certifying the
number of shares owned shall be issued to each stockholder
in such form not inconsistent with the Certificate of Incorporation as shall be approved by the Board of Directors.

Such certificates of stock shall be numbered and registered
in the order in which they are issued and shall be signed
by the President or a Vice President, and by the Secretary
or an Assistant Secretary; provided, however, that where such
certificates are signed by a transfer agent or a transfer
clerk acting on behalf of the corporation and a registrar,
the signatures of the President and Secretary may be facsimile.
In case any officer or officers who shall have signed or
whose facsimile signature shall have been used on any such
certificate or certificates shall cease to be such officer
or officers of the corporation, whether because of death,
resignation or otherwise, before such certificate or certificates shall have been delivered by the corporation, such
certificate or certificates may nevertheless be adopted by the
corporation and be issued and delivered as though the person
or persons who signed such certificate or certificates or whose
facsimile signature or signatures shall have been used
thereon had not ceased to be such officer or officers of
the corporation.

Transfers of Shares

SECTION 2 -- Transfers of shares shall be made only
upon the books of the corporation by the holder, in person,
or by power of attorney duly executed and filed with the
Secretary of the corporation, and on the surrender of the
certificate or certificates of such shares, properly assigned.

Lost, Stolen, or Destroyed Certificates

SECTION 3 -- No certificate for shares of the capital
stock of the corporation shall be issued in place of any
certificate alleged to have been lost, stolen, or destroyed,
except by order of the Board of Directors and on delivery
to the corporation of a bond of indemnity in an amount satis-
factory to the Board of Directors executed by the person to
whom the stock should be issued and also by an approved surety
company, against any claim upon or in respect of such lost,
stolen, or destroyed certificate. Proper and legal evidence
of such loss, theft or destruction shall be produced to the
Board, if required. The Board of Directors, in its discretion,
may refuse to issue such new certificate, save upon the order
of some court having jurisdiction in such matters.

Transfer Agent and Registrar; Regulations

SECTION 4 -- The corporation shall, if and whenever
the Board of Directors shall so determine, maintain one or
more transfer offices or agencies, each in charge of a trans-

fer agent designated by the Board of Directors, where the shares of the capital stock of the corporation shall be directly transferable, or a transfer clerk to act on behalf of the Corporation in connection with such transfers, and also one or more registry offices, each in charge of a registrar designated by the Board of Directors, where such shares of stock shall be registered, and no certificate for shares of the capital stock of the corporation in respect of which a transfer agent or transfer clerk and registrar shall have been designated, shall be valid unless countersigned by such transfer agent or transfer clerk and registered by such registrar. The Board of Directors may also make such additional rules and regulations as it may deem expedient concerning the issue, transfer and registration of certificates for shares of the capital stock of the corporation.

Closing of Transfer Books

SECTION 5 -- The Board of Directors may fix the time, not exceeding forty days preceding the date of any meeting of stockholders or any dividend payment date or any date for the allotment of rights, or the date when any change or conversion or exchange of capital stock shall go into effect, during which the books of the corporation shall be closed against transfers of stock, and may close such transfer books for a period of not exceeding forty days in connection with obtaining the consent of stockholders for any purpose. In lieu of providing for the closing of books against transfers of stock as aforesaid, the Board of Directors from time to time, and at any time, may fix in advance a date, not exceeding forty days preceding the date of any meeting of stockholders or the date for the payment of any dividend or the date for any allotment of rights, or the date when any change or conversion or exchange of capital stock shall go into effect, or a date in connection with obtaining such consent, as a record date for the determination of the stockholders entitled to notice of and to vote at such meeting or entitled to receive such dividends or allotment or rights, or to exercise the rights in respect of any such change, conversion or exchange of capital stock, or to give such consent, as the case may be; and only stockholders of record on such date shall be entitled to notice of or to vote at such meeting or to receive such dividends or allotment of rights, or to exercise the rights in respect of any such change, conversion or exchange of capital stock, or to give such consent, as the case may be.

Article VI

DIVIDENDS AND RESERVES

Dividends upon the capital stock of the corporation
may be declared as permitted by law by the Board of Directors
at any regular or special meeting. Before payment of any
dividend or making any distribution of profits, there may be
set aside out of the surplus or net profits of the corporation
such sum or sums as the Board of Directors, from time to time,
in its absolute discretion, thinks proper as a reserve fund
to meet contingencies, or for such other purposes as the
Board shall think conducive to the interests of the corporation, and any reserve so established may be abolished and
restored to the surplus account by like action of the Board.

Article VII

SEAL

The Seal of the corporation shall bear the corporate
name of the corporation, the year of its incorporation
and the words "Corporate Seal, Delaware".

Article VIII

WAIVER

Whenever any notice whatever is required to be given
by statute or under the provisions of the Certificate of Incorporation or By-Laws of the corporation, a waiver thereof
in writing signed by the person or persons entitled to such
notice, whether before or after the time stated therein,
shall be deemed equivalent thereto.

Article IX

FISCAL YEAR

The fiscal year of the corporation shall begin with
January first and end with December thirty-first.

Article X

AMENDMENTS

The Board of Directors from time to time shall have the power to make, alter, amend, or repeal any and all of the By-Laws, but any By-Laws so made, altered, amended or repealed by the Board of Directors may be amended, altered or repealed by the stockholders.

C. SAMPLE MINUTES

MINUTES OF

SPECIAL MEETING OF THE BOARD OF DIRECTORS

OF

ANONYMOUS OIL CORPORATION

HELD

FEBRUARY 16, 1972

A special meeting of the Board of Directors of Anonymous Oil Corporation was held at 10:00 o'clock A.M., Eastern Standard Time, at the offices of the Corporation, 2169 Emerson Avenue, Braintree, Massachusetts.

The following directors, constituting a quorum, were present at the meeting:

Daniel Drew
James Fisk
Henriette Green
Ivar Kreuger
Charles Ponzi

The following directors were absent:

Joaquin Murietta
Jack Sheppard

Mr. Fisk, President of the Corporation, acted as Chairman of the meeting and Edward Gibbon, Secretary, recorded the minutes thereof.

The Secretary presented to the meeting the original Call therefor signed by the President and the original Waiver of Notice and Consent to said meeting signed by all the directors of the Corporation. Upon motion duly made, seconded and unanimously carried, the Call and Waiver of Notice and Consent were made a part of the records of the Corporation and of this meeting, and the Secretary was directed to attach the same to the minutes.

The Chairman called the meeting to order and proceeded with the first item of business on the agenda. The Chairman presented to the meeting a proposed form of Bank Loan Agreement between the Corporation and The Last National City Bank of Erewhon providing for loans to the Corporation in an amount not exceeding $2,000,000. The Chairman explained the terms of the proposed Agreement. Said document was ordered filed with the records of the Corporation.

After discussions, on motion duly made, seconded and unanimously carried, it was

> RESOLVED, That the Bank Loan Agreement in the form presented to this meeting between the Corporation and The Last City National Bank of Erewhon be and the same is hereby approved, and the officers of this corporation be and they hereby are authorized and directed on behalf of this Corporation to enter into such Bank Loan Agreement in such form, with such changes as such officers may approve, such approval to be evidenced conclusively by their execution of said agreement; and further

> RESOLVED, That the officers of the Corporation be and they hereby are authorized to take any and all action necessary or appropriate to carry out the terms and provisions of said Bank Loan Agreement in the form of which the same shall be executed; and further

> RESOLVED, That the President, any Vice President, the Treasurer and the Secretary of the Corporation, or any of them, be and thus hereby are authorized to sign notes and any certificate or other documents required by said agreement to be furnished to said Bank.

There being no further business, upon motion duly made and seconded and unanimously voted, the meeting was adjourned.

_____
Secretary

APPROVED:

_____
Chairman

Vagts Basic Corp.Law 2nd Ed. UCB—2
1983 Supp.

D.   SAMPLE STOCK CERTIFICATE

General Dynamics Corporation will furnish without charge, to each stockholder who so requests, a statement of the powers, designations, preferences and relative, participating, optional or other special rights of each class of stock or series thereof of the Corporation, and the qualifications, limitations or restrictions of such powers, designations, preferences and/or rights. Such request may be made to the Corporation at its executive offices in the City of New York or to the Transfer Agent countersigning this Certificate, at its head office.

For Value Received _____ *hereby sell, assign, and transfer unto*

_____

(PLEASE PRINT OR TYPEWRITE NAME AND ADDRESS OF ASSIGNEE)

_____

_____

_____ *Shares*

of the capital stock represented by the within Certificate, and do hereby irrevocably constitute and appoint

_____ *Attorney,*

to transfer the said stock on the books of the within named Corporation, with full power of substitution in the premises.

Dated _____

NOTICE: The Signature to this Assignment must correspond with the name as written upon the face of the Certificate in every particular, without alteration or enlargement or any change whatever

_____

E. SAMPLE PROXY FORM

The shares represented by this proxy will be voted as directed by the stockholder. If no direction is given when the duly executed proxy is returned, such shares will be voted "FOR" Proposals 1 and 2 and "AGAINST" Proposals 3, 4 and 5.

```
         981
 001210 60705910 VAGTS----DORO-80900000001920000000008455
```

The Board of Directors Recommends a Vote FOR Items 1 and 2		
Item 1 — Election of directors: G.A. Birrell, L.M. Branscomb, H.L. Clark, A. Greenspan, S.C. Johnson, W.J. Kennedy III, J.S. Lafontant, A.H. Massad, L.L. Morgan, A.E. Murray, S.S. Olayan, A.J.F. O'Reilly, J.Q. Riordan, H. Schmertz, W.W. Scranton, E.B. Sheldon, W.P. Tavoulareas, R.F. Tucker, R. Warner, Jr., P.J. Wolfe, L.M. Woods		**Item 2** — Ratification of Independent Auditors
For Withheld for all Withheld for the following only: (Write the nominee's name in the space below)		For Against Abstain
O O O _____		O O O

The Board of Directors Recommends a Vote AGAINST Items 3, 4 and 5		
Item 3 — Preemptive rights	**Item 4** — Stockholder nominations for directors	**Item 5** — Corporate acquisitions
For Against Abstain	For Against Abstain	For Against Abstain
O O O	O O O	O O O

```
┌ MRS DOROTHY VAGTS              ┐
  HARVARD LAW SCHOOL
  LANGDELL HALL
  CAMBRIDGE 38 MASS   02138
└                               ┘
```

Date _____

Signature _____

Signature _____

Please date and sign as your name appears above and return in the enclosed envelope. If acting as executor, administrator, trustee, guardian, etc., you should so indicate when signing. If the signer is a corporation, please sign the full corporate name, by duly authorized officer. If shares are held jointly, each stockholder named should sign.

[C6858]

Mobil Corporation   **proxy**

SOLICITED BY THE BOARD OF DIRECTORS for Annual Meeting of Stockholders

TUPPERWARE CONVENTION CENTER AUDITORIUM
ORANGE BLOSSOM TRAIL
ORLANDO, FLORIDA 32802
THURSDAY, MAY 6, 1982, AT 10:00 A.M.

The undersigned hereby appoints Rawleigh Warner, Jr., William P. Tavoulareas and Margaret M. Day, and any one of them, each with power of substitution, the attorneys of the undersigned to vote all shares held of record on the record date by the undersigned, as directed and, in their discretion, on all other matters which may properly come before the 1982 Annual Meeting of Stockholders of Mobil Corporation, or any adjournment thereof.

The undersigned directs said proxies to vote as specified upon the items shown on the reverse side, which are referred to in the Notice of Annual Meeting and set forth in the Proxy Statement.

(Continued, and to be signed, on the reverse side)

[C8857]

F.   SAMPLE PROSPECTUS (First three pages only)

PROSPECTUS

ñ|s nutri/system, inc.

700,000 Shares
COMMON STOCK

Of the shares offered hereby, the Underwriters are acquiring 100,000 shares from the Company and 600,000 shares from the Selling Shareholder. See "Principal and Selling Shareholder."

On January 11, 1983, the closing price of the Common Stock on the New York Stock Exchange was $36.25. The Common Stock is traded under the symbol NTR.

THESE SECURITIES HAVE NOT BEEN APPROVED OR DISAPPROVED BY THE SECURITIES AND EXCHANGE COMMISSION NOR HAS THE COMMISSION PASSED UPON THE ACCURACY OR ADEQUACY OF THIS PROSPECTUS. ANY REPRESENTATION TO THE CONTRARY IS A CRIMINAL OFFENSE.

	Price to Public	Underwriting Discounts and Commissions (1)	Proceeds to Company (2)	Proceeds to Selling Shareholder (2)
Per Share	$36.25	$1.92	$34.33	$34.33
Total (3)				
Minimum	$25,375,000	$1,344,000	$3,433,000	$20,598,000
Maximum	$27,912,500	$1,478,400	$3,433,000	$23,001,100

(1) See "Underwriting."
(2) Before deducting expenses payable by the Company estimated at $49,200 and expenses payable by the Selling Shareholder estimated at $275,800.
(3) The Selling Shareholder has granted the Underwriters a seven-day option to purchase up to 70,000 additional shares to cover over-allotments. See "Underwriting." In the foregoing table the minimum amounts assume that the option will not be exercised and the maximum amounts assume that the option will be exercised in full.

The shares of Common Stock are offered by the Underwriters subject to receipt and acceptance of such shares by them. The Underwriters reserve the right to reject any order in whole or in part. It is expected that delivery of the certificates for the shares will be made against payment therefor on or about January 19, 1983.

L. F. ROTHSCHILD, UNTERBERG, TOWBIN

The date of this Prospectus is January 12, 1983.

[C6859]

No dealer, salesperson or other person has been authorized to give any information or to make any representation not contained in this Prospectus in connection with the offer made hereby. If given or made, such information or representation must not be relied upon as having been authorized by the Company, the Selling Shareholder or any Underwriter. This prospectus does not constitute an offer of any securities other than the Common Stock to which it relates or an offer to any person in any jurisdiction where such an offer would be unlawful. Neither delivery of this Prospectus nor any sale made hereunder shall under any circumstances create an implication that information contained herein is correct as of any time subsequent to the date hereof.

TABLE OF CONTENTS

The Company is subject to the informational requirements of the Securities Exchange Act of 1934 and in accordance therewith has filed reports and other information with the Securities and Exchange Commission. Information, as of particular dates, concerning the Company's directors and officers, their remuneration, options granted to them, the principal holders of securities of the Company and any material interest of such persons in transactions with the Company is set forth in proxy statements distributed to shareholders of the Company and filed with the Commission. Such reports, proxy statements, and other information filed by the Company can be inspected and copies made at the offices of the Commission at Judiciary Plaza, 450 Fifth Street, N.W., Washington, D.C. 20549, and the Commission's Regional Offices in Chicago (219 South Dearborn Street, Chicago, Illinois 60604), Los Angeles (10960 Wilshire Boulevard, Los Angeles, California 90024), and New York (26 Federal Plaza, New York, New York 10007); copies of such material may be obtained from the Public Reference Section of the Commission, Washington, D.C. 20549 at prescribed rates. The Company's Common Stock is listed on the New York Stock Exchange. Reports, proxy statements and other information concerning the Company have been filed with and may be inspected at the New York Stock Exchange.

IN CONNECTION WITH THIS OFFERING, THE UNDERWRITERS MAY OVER-ALLOT OR EFFECT TRANSACTIONS WHICH STABILIZE OR MAINTAIN THE MARKET PRICE OF THE COMMON STOCK OF THE COMPANY AT A LEVEL ABOVE THAT WHICH MIGHT OTHERWISE PREVAIL IN THE OPEN MARKET. SUCH TRANSACTIONS MAY BE EFFECTED ON THE NEW YORK STOCK EXCHANGE, THE PHILADELPHIA STOCK EXCHANGE OR OTHERWISE. SUCH STABILIZING, IF COMMENCED, MAY BE DISCONTINUED AT ANY TIME.

[C6860]

PROSPECTUS SUMMARY

The following summary is qualified in its entirety by the more detailed information and financial statements appearing elsewhere in this Prospectus. All share data in this Prospectus have been adjusted to reflect a two-for-one stock split in August 1981 and a three-for-two stock split in August 1982.

The Offering

	Minimum	Maximum
Shares offered by Company	100,000	100,000
Shares offered by Selling Shareholder	600,000	670,000
Shares to be outstanding after the offering	9,690,651	9,690,651
Use of proceeds		Working capital and general corporate purposes, including opening and acquiring weight loss/figure control centers

Business

The Company owns and operates weight loss/figure control centers and franchises to others the right to use its name and programs. Its prepackaged, premeasured foods are sold to participants in its programs at Company-owned and at franchised centers. The Company believes it is one of the largest companies in the United States in the weight loss/figure control field. The Company also operates and franchises cosmetics and skin care retail stores and an executive recruiting and outplacement service.

Summary Financial Information
(in thousands, except per share data)

Income Statement Data:

	Year Ended July 31,					Three Months Ended October 31,	
	1978	1979	1980	1981	1982[1]	1981	1982
						(unaudited)	
Revenues	$6,050	$15,023	$23,204	$49,183	$124,648	$21,724	$46,232
Income from continuing operations[2]	497	2,776	4,052	9,247	18,085	3,762	5,562
Per share data:							
Income from continuing operations[2]	.05	.31	.45	1.00	1.91	.40	.58
Cash dividends declared	.003	.01	.06	.06	.17	.033	.06
Average number of shares .	9,000	9,000	9,000	9,206	9,485	9,452	9,625

Balance Sheet Data:

	July 31,					October 31, 1982	
	1978	1979	1980	1981	1982	Actual	As adjusted[3]
						(unaudited)	
Working capital	$1,127	$3,719	$ 4,912	$12,113	$ (2,943)	$ (874)	$ 2,510
Tangible assets	3,312	8,303	12,028	29,239	41,545	53,220	56,604
Total assets	3,312	8,594	12,848	30,156	69,194	81,382	84,766
Long-term debt	317	237	86	-0-	-0-	8,378	8,378
Shareholders' equity	1,086	3,872	7,046	17,775	36,952	42,403	45,786

[1] The Company made significant acquisitions in 1982. For fiscal 1982, on a pro forma basis (adjusted to reflect such acquisitions as if they had been made August 1, 1980) revenues were $154,894,000, net income was $15,443,000 and net income per share was $1.63. See Note C to the Company's Consolidated Financial Statements and the Unaudited Pro Forma Combined Statements of Income.

[2] Before extraordinary credit of $222,000 ($.02 per share) in 1979.

[3] Adjusted to reflect the sale of the shares offered by the Company hereby, and the anticipated use of net proceeds.

FEDERAL STATUTES AND R

A. THE SECURITIES ACT OF 193~~5~~ (EXCERPTS)

§ 2. DEFINITIONS

When used in this title, unless the context otherwise requires—

(1) The term "security" means any note, stock, treasury stock, bond, debenture, evidence of indebtedness, certificate of interest or participation in any profit-sharing agreement, collateral-trust certificate, preorganization certificate or subscription, transferable share, investment contract, voting-trust certificate, certificate of deposit for a security, fractional undivided interest in oil, gas, or other mineral rights, or, in general, any interest or instrument commonly known as a "security," or any certificate of interest or participation in, temporary or interim certificate for, receipt for, guarantee of, or warrant or right to subscribe to or purchase, any of the foregoing. . . .

(3) The term "sale" or "sell" shall include every contract of sale or disposition of a security or interest in a security, for value. The term "offer to sell," "offer for sale," or "offer" shall include every attempt or offer to dispose of, or solicitation of an offer to buy, a security or interest in a security, for value. The terms defined in this paragraph and the term "offer to buy" as used in subsection (c) of section 5 shall not include preliminary negotiations or agreements between an issuer (or any person directly or indirectly controlling or controlled by an issuer, or under direct or indirect common control with an issuer) and any underwriter or among underwriters who are or are to be in privity of contract with an issuer (or any person directly or indirectly controlling or controlled by an issuer, or under direct or indirect common control with an issuer).

(4) The term "issuer" means every person who issues or proposes to issue any security;

(11) The term "underwriter" means any person who has purchased from an issuer with a view to, or offers or sells for an issuer in connection with, the distribution of any security, or participates or has a direct or indirect participation in any such undertaking, or participates or has a participation in the direct or indirect underwriting of any such undertaking; but such term shall not include a person whose interest is limited to a commission from an underwriter or dealer not in excess of the usual and customary distributors' or sellers' commission.

1. 15 U.S.C.A. § 77a et seq.

, The term "accredited investor" shall mean—

.) a bank . . . whether acting in its individual or fiduciary capaci-
.y; an insurance company . . .; an investment company registered
under the Investment Company Act of 1940 or a business development company as defined in section 2(a)(48) of that Act; a Small Business Investment Company licensed by the Small Business Administration; or an
employee benefit plan, including an individual retirement account, which
is subject to the provisions of the Employee Retirement Income Security
Act of 1974, if the investment decision is made by a plan fiduciary, . . .,
which is either a bank, insurance company, or registered investment adviser;
or

(ii) any person who, on the basis of such factors as financial sophistica-
tion, net worth, knowledge, and experience in financial matters, or amount
of assets under management qualifies as an accredited investor under rules
and regulations which the Commission shall prescribe.

§ 3. EXEMPTED SECURITIES

(a) Except as hereinafter expressly provided, the provisions of this title
shall not apply to any of the following classes of securities:

. . .

(11) Any security which is a part of an issue offered and sold only to
persons resident within a single State or Territory, where the issuer of such
security is a person resident and doing business within, or, if a corporation,
incorporated by and doing business within, such State or Territory.

(b) The Commission may from time to time by its rules and regulations,
and subject to such terms and conditions as may be prescribed therein, add
any class of securities to the securities exempted as provided in this section,
if it finds that the enforcement of this title with respect to such securities
is not necessary in the public interest and for the protection of investors by
reason of the small amount involved or the limited character of the public
offering; but no issue of securities shall be exempted under this subsection
where the aggregate amount at which such issue is offered to the public
exceeds $5,000,000.[2]

(c) The Commission may from time to time by its rules and regulations
and subject to such terms and conditions as may be prescribed therein, add
to the securities exempted as provided in this section any class of securities
issued by a small business investment company under the Small Business
Investment Act of 1958 if it finds, having regard to the purposes of that
Act, that the enforcement of this Act with respect to such securities is not
necessary in the public interest and for the protection of investors.

---

2. This authority has been exercised by
the SEC in Regulation A, which permits small issues to by-pass some, but
not all, of the requirements generally
applicable.

§ 4. EXEMPTED TRANSACTIONS

The provisions of section 5 shall not apply to—

(1) transactions by any person other than an issuer, underwriter, or dealer.

(2) transactions by an issuer not involving any public offering.

(3) transactions by a dealer (including an underwriter no longer acting as an underwriter in respect of the security involved in such transaction), except—

(A) transactions taking place prior to the expiration of forty days after the first date upon which the security was bona fide offered to the public by the issuer or by or through an underwriter,

(B) transactions in a security as to which a registration statement has been filed taking place prior to the expiration of forty days after the effective date of such registration statement or prior to the expiration of forty days after the first date upon which the security was bona fide offered to the public by the issuer or by or through an underwriter after such effective date, whichever is later (excluding in the computation of such forty days any time during which a stop order issued under section 8 is in effect as to the security), or such shorter period as the Commission may specify by rules and regulations or order, and

(C) transactions as to securities constituting the whole or a part of an unsold allotment to or subscription by such dealer as a participant in the distribution of such securities by the issuer or by or through an underwriter.

With respect to transactions referred to in clause (B), if securities of the issuer have not previously been sold pursuant to an earlier effective registration statement the applicable period, instead of forty days, shall be ninety days, or such shorter period as the Commission may specify by rules and regulations or order.

(4) brokers' transactions executed upon customers' orders on any exchange or in the over-the-counter market but not the solicitation of such orders.

. . .

(6) transactions involving offers or sales by an issuer solely to one or more accredited investors, if the aggregate offering price of an issue of securities offered in reliance on this paragraph does not exceed the amount allowed under section 3(b), if there is no advertising or public solicitation in connection with the transaction by the issuer or anyone acting on the issuer's behalf, and if the issuer files such notice with the Commission as the Commission shall prescribe.

§ 5. PROHIBITIONS RELATING TO INTERSTATE COMMERCE AND THE MAILS

(a) Unless a registration statement is in effect as to a security, it shall be unlawful for any person, directly or indirectly—

(1) to make use of any means or instruments of transportation or communication in interstate commerce or of the mails to sell such security through the use or medium of any prospectus or otherwise; or

(2) to carry or cause to be carried through the mails or in interstate commerce, by any means or instruments of transportation, any such security for the purpose of sale or for delivery after sale.

(b) It shall be unlawful for any person, directly or indirectly—

(1) to make use of any means or instruments of transportation or communication in interstate commerce or of the mails to carry or transmit any prospectus relating to any security with respect to which a registration statement has been filed under this title, unless such prospectus meets the requirements of section 10; or

(2) to carry or cause to be carried through the mails or in interstate commerce any such security for the purpose of sale or for delivery after sale, unless accompanied or preceded by a prospectus that meets the requirements of subsection (a) of section 10.

(c) It shall be unlawful for any person, directly or indirectly, to make use of any means or instruments of transportation or communication in interstate commerce or of the mails to offer to sell or offer to buy through the use or medium of any prospectus or otherwise any security, unless a registration statement has been filed as to such security, or while the registration statement is the subject of a refusal order or stop order or (prior to the effective date of the registration statement) any public proceeding or examination under section 8.

§ 11. CIVIL LIABILITIES ON ACCOUNT OF FALSE REGISTRATION STATEMENT

(a) In case any part of the registration statement, when such part became effective, contained an untrue statement of a material fact or omitted to state a material fact required to be stated therein or necessary to make the statements therein not misleading, any person acquiring such security (unless it is proved that at the time of such acquisition he knew of such untruth or omission) may, either at law or in equity, in any court of competent jurisdiction, sue—

(1) every person who signed the registration statement[3];

(2) every person who was a director of (or person performing similar functions) or partner in, the issuer at the time of the filing of the part of the registration statement with respect to which his liability is asserted;

(3) every person who, with his consent, is named in the registration statement as being or about to become a director, person performing similar functions, or partner;

3. Section 6(a) requires that the registration statement be signed by "each issuer, its principal executive officer or officers, its principal financial officer, its comptroller or principal accounting officer, and the majority of its board of directors or persons performing similar functions . . ."

(4) every accountant, engineer, or appraiser, or any person whose profession gives authority to a statement made by him, who has with his consent been named as having prepared or certified any part of the registration statement, or as having prepared or certified any report or valuation which is used in connection with the registration statement, with respect to the statement in such registration statement, report, or valuation, which purports to have been prepared or certified by him;

(5) every underwriter with respect to such security.

If such person acquired the security after the issuer has made generally available to its security holders an earning statement covering a period of at least twelve months beginning after the effective date of the registration statement, then the right of recovery under this subsection shall be conditioned on proof that such person acquired the security relying upon such untrue statement in the registration statement or relying upon the registration statement and not knowing of such omission, but such reliance may be established without proof of the reading of the registration statement by such person.

(b) Notwithstanding the provisions of subsection (a) no person, other than the issuer, shall be liable as provided therein who shall sustain the burden of proof—

(1) that before the effective date of the part of the registration statement with respect to which his liability is asserted (A) he had resigned from or had taken such steps as are permitted by law to resign from, or ceased or refused to act in, every office, capacity, or relationship in which he was described in the registration statement as acting or agreeing to act, and (B) he had advised the Commission and the issuer in writing that he had taken such action and that he would not be responsible for such part of the registration statement; or

(2) that if such part of the registration statement became effective without his knowledge, upon becoming aware of such fact he forthwith acted and advised the Commission, in accordance with paragraph (1), and, in addition, gave reasonable public notice that such part of the registration statement had become effective without his knowledge; or

(3) that (A) as regards any part of the registration statement not purporting to be made on the authority of an expert, and not purporting to be a copy of or extract from a report or valuation of an expert, and not purporting to be made on the authority of a public official document or statement, he had, after reasonable investigation, reasonable ground to believe and did believe, at the time such part of the registration statement became effective, that the statements therein were true and that there was no omission to state a material fact required to be stated therein or necessary to make the statements therein not misleading; and (B) as regards any part of the registration statement purporting to be made upon his authority as an expert or purporting to be a copy of or extract from a report or valuation of himself as an expert, (i) he had, after reasonable investigation, reasonable ground to believe and did believe, at the time such part of the registra-

tion statement became effective, that the statements therein were true and that there was no omission to state a material fact required to be stated therein or necessary to make the statements therein not misleading, or (ii) such part of the registration statement did not fairly represent his statement as an expert or was not a fair copy of or extract from his report or valuation as an expert; and (C) as regards any part of the registration statement purporting to be made on the authority of an expert (other than himself) or purporting to be a copy of or extract from a report or valuation of an expert (other than himself), he had no reasonable ground to believe, and did not believe, at the time such part of the registration statement became effective, that the statements therein were untrue or that there was an omission to state a material fact required to be stated therein or necessary to make the statements therein not misleading, or that such part of the registration statement did not fairly represent the statement of the expert or was not a fair copy of or extract from the report or valuation of the expert; . . .

(c) In determining, for the purpose of paragraph (3) of subsection (b) of this section, what constitutes reasonable investigation and reasonable ground for belief, the standard of reasonableness shall be that required of a prudent man in the management of his own property.

. . .

(e) The suit authorized under subsection (a) may be to recover such damages as shall represent the difference between the amount paid for the security (not exceeding the price at which the security was offered to the public) and (1) the value thereof as of the time such suit was brought, or (2) the price at which such security shall have been disposed of in the market before suit, or (3) the price at which such security shall have been disposed of after suit but before judgment if such damages shall be less than the damages representing the difference between the amount paid for the security (not exceeding the price at which the security was offered to the public) and the value thereof as of the time such suit was brought: Provided, that if the defendant proves that any portion or all of such damages represents other than the depreciation in value of such security resulting from such part of the registration statement, with respect to which his liability is asserted, not being true or omitting to state a material fact required to be stated therein or necessary to make the statements therein not misleading, such portion of or all such damages shall not be recoverable. In no event shall any underwriter (unless such underwriter shall have knowingly received from the issuer for acting as an underwriter some benefit, directly or indirectly, in which all other underwriters similarly situated did not share in proportion to their respective interests in the underwriting) be liable in any suit or as a consequence of suits authorized under subsection (a) for damages in excess of the total price at which the securities underwritten by him and distributed to the public were offered to the public. In any suit under this or any other section of this title the court may, in its discretion, require an undertaking for the payment of the costs of such suit, including reasonable attorney's fees, and if judgment shall be rendered against a party litigant, upon the motion of the other party litigant, such costs may be assessed in favor of such party litigant (whether or not such undertaking has been required) if the court believes the suit or the defense to have been without merit, in an amount sufficient to reimburse him for the reasonable expenses incurred by him, in connection with such suit, such costs to be taxed in the manner usually provided for taxing of costs in the court in which the suit was heard.

(f) All or any one or more of the persons specified in subsection (a) shall be jointly and severally liable, and every person who becomes liable to make any payment under this section may recover contribution as in cases of contract from any person who, if sued separately, would have been liable to make the same payment, unless the person who has become liable was, and the other was not, guilty of fraudulent misrepresentation.

(g) In no case shall the amount recoverable under this section exceed the price at which the security was offered to the public.

§ 12. CIVIL LIABILITIES ARISING IN CONNECTION WITH PROSPECTUSES AND COMMUNICATIONS

Any person who—

(1) offers or sells a security in violation of section 5, or

(2) offers or sells a security (whether or not exempted by the provisions of section 3, other than paragraph (2) of subsection (a) thereof), by the use of any means or instruments of transportation or communication in interstate commerce or of the mails, by means of a prospectus or oral communication, which includes an untrue statement of a material fact or omits to state a material fact necessary in order to make the statements, in the light of the circumstances under which they were made, not misleading (the purchaser not knowing of such untruth or omission), and who shall not sustain the burden of proof that he did not know, and in the exercise of reasonable care could not have known, of such untruth or omission,

shall be liable to the person purchasing such security from him, who may sue either at law or in equity in any court of competent jurisdiction, to recover the consideration paid for such security with interest thereon, less the amount of any income received thereon, upon the tender of such security, or for damages if he no longer owns the security.

§ 17. FRAUDULENT INTERSTATE TRANSACTIONS

(a) It shall be unlawful for any person in the offer or sale of any securities by the use of any means or instruments of transportation or communication in interstate commerce or by the use of the mails, directly or indirectly—

(1) to employ any device, scheme or artifice to defraud, or

(2) to obtain money or property by means of any untrue statement of a material fact or any omission to state a material fact necessary in order to make the statements made, in the light of the circumstances under which they were made, not misleading, or

(3) to engage in any transaction, practice, or course of business which operates or would operate as a fraud or deceit upon the purchaser.

(b) It shall be unlawful for any person, by the use of any means or instruments of transportation or communication in interstate commerce or by the use of the mails, to publish, give publicity to, or circulate any notice, circular, advertisement, newspaper, article, letter, investment service, or communication which, though not purporting to offer a security for sale, describes such security for a consideration received or to be received, directly or indirectly, from an issuer, underwriter, or dealer, without fully disclosing the receipt, whether past or prospective, of such consideration and the amount thereof.

(c) The exemptions provided in section 3 shall not apply to the provisions of this section.

B. THE SECURITIES EXCHANGE ACT OF 1934 (EXCERPTS) [4]

§ 3. DEFINITIONS AND APPLICATION OF TITLE

(a) When used in this title, unless the context otherwise requires—

(1) The term "exchange" means any organization, association, or group of persons, whether incorporated or unincorporated, which constitutes, maintains, or provides a market place or facilities for bringing together purchasers and sellers of securities or for otherwise performing with respect to securities the functions commonly performed by a stock exchange as that term is generally understood, and includes the market place and the market facilities maintained by such exchange.

.   .   .

(4) The term "broker" means any person engaged in the business of effecting transactions in securities for the account of others, but does not include a bank.

(5) The term "dealer" means any person engaged in the business of buying and selling securities for his own account, through a broker or otherwise, but does not include a bank, or any person insofar as he buys or sells securities for his own account, either individually or in some fiduciary capacity, but not as a part of a regular business.

.   .   .

(7) The term "director" means any director of a corporation or any person performing similar functions with respect to any organization, whether incorporated or unincorporated.

.   .   .

(9) The term "person" means a natural person, company, government or political subdivision, agency or instrumentality of a government.

(10) The term "security" means any note, stock, treasury stock, bond, debenture, certificate of interest or participation in any profit-sharing agreement or in any oil, gas, or other mineral royalty or lease, any collateral-trust certificate, preorganization certificate or subscription, transferable

---

4. 15 U.S.C.A. § 78a et seq.

share, investment contract, voting-trust certificate, certificate of deposit, for a security, or in general, any instrument commonly known as a "security"; or any certificate of interest or participation in, temporary or interim certificate for, receipt for, or warrant or right to subscribe to or purchase, any of the foregoing; but shall not include currency or any note, draft, bill of exchange, or banker's acceptance which has a maturity at the time of issuance of not exceeding nine months, exclusive of days of grace, or any renewal thereof the maturity of which is likewise limited.

(11) The term "equity security" means any stock or similar security; or any security convertible, with or without consideration, into such a security, or carrying any warrant or right to subscribe to or purchase such a security; or any such warrant or right; or any other security which the Commission shall deem to be of similar nature and consider necessary or appropriate, by such rules and regulations as it may prescribe in the public interest or for the protection of investors, to treat as an equity security.

. . .

§ 10. REGULATION OF THE USE OF MANIPULATIVE AND DECEPTIVE DEVICES

It shall be unlawful for any person, directly or indirectly, by the use of any means or instrumentality of interstate commerce or of the mails, or of any facility of any national securities exchange—

(a) To effect a short sale, or to use or employ any stop-loss order in connection with the purchase or sale, of any security registered on a national securities exchange, in contravention of such rules and regulations as the Commission may prescribe as necessary or appropriate in the public interest or for the protection of investors.

(b) To use or employ, in connection with the purchase or sale of any security registered on a national securities exchange or any security not so registered, any manipulative or deceptive device or contrivance in contravention of such rules and regulations as the Commission may prescribe as necessary or appropriate in the public interest or for the protection of investors.

§ 12. REGISTRATION REQUIREMENTS FOR SECURITIES

(a) It shall be unlawful for any member, broker, or dealer to effect any transaction in any security (other than an exempted security) on a national securities exchange unless a registration [5] is effective as to such security for such exchange in accordance with the provisions of this title and the rules and regulations thereunder.

(b) A security may be registered on a national securities exchange by the issuer filing an application with the exchange (and filing with the Commission such duplicate originals thereof as the Commission may require), which application shall contain—

---

5. Note that "registration" of a newly issued security under the Securities Act of 1933 is separate and distinct from this "registration."

(1) Such information, in such detail, as to the issuer and any person directly or indirectly controlling or controlled by, or under direct or indirect common control with, the issuer, and any guarantor of the security as to principal or interest or both, as the Commission may by rules and regulations require, as necessary or appropriate in the public interest or for the protection of investors, in respect of the following:

(A) the organization, financial structure and nature of the business;

(B) the terms, position, rights, and privileges of the different classes of securities outstanding;

(C) the terms on which their securities are to be, and during the preceding three years have been, offered to the public or otherwise;

(D) the directors, officers, and underwriters, and each security holder of record holding more than 10 per centum of any class of any equity security of the issuer (other than an exempted security), their remuneration and their interests in the securities of, and their material contracts with, the issuer and any person directly or indirectly controlling or controlled by, or under direct or indirect common control with, the issuer;

(E) remuneration to others than directors and officers exceeding $20,000 per annum;

(F) bonus and profit-sharing arrangements;

(G) management and service contracts;

(H) options existing or to be created in respect of their securities;

(I) material contracts, not made in the ordinary course of business,   .   .   .

(g)(1) Every issuer which is engaged in interstate commerce, or in a business affecting interstate commerce, or whose securities are traded by use of the mails or any means or instrumentality of interstate commerce shall—

(A) within one hundred and twenty days after the last day of its first fiscal year ended after the effective date of this subsection on which the issuer has total assets exceeding $1,000,000 and a class of equity security (other than an exempted security) held of record by seven hundred and fifty or more persons; and

(B) within one hundred and twenty days after the last day of its first fiscal year ended after two years from the effective date of this subsection on which the issuer has total assets exceeding $1,000,000 and a class of equity security (other than an exempted security) held of record by five hundred or more but less than seven hundred and fifty persons,[6]

register such security by filing with the Commission a registration statement (and such copies thereof as the Commission may require) with respect to

6. Students find this confusing; it is a transitional measure designed to lower the threshold of Section 12's applicability first to 750 and then to 500, where it has been since 1966. In April 1982, the Commission exercised its exempting and rule-making powers to relieve issuers with less than $3,000,000 in total assets from the registration requirement.

such security containing such information and documents as the Commission may specify comparable to that which is required in an application to register a security pursuant to subsection (b) of this section.

.   .   .

§ 13. PERIODICAL AND OTHER REPORTS

(a) Every issuer of a security registered pursuant to section 12 of this title shall file with the Commission, in accordance with such rules and regulations as the Commission may prescribe as necessary or appropriate for the proper protection of investors and to insure fair dealing in the security—

(1) Such information and documents (and such copies thereof) as the Commission shall require to keep reasonably current the information and documents required to be included in or filed with an application or registration statement filed pursuant to section 12, except that the Commission may not require the filing of any material contract wholly executed before July 1, 1962.

(2) Such annual reports (and such copies thereof), certified if required by the rules and regulations of the Commission by independent public accountants, and such quarterly reports (and such copies thereof), as the Commission may prescribe.

Every issuer of a security registered on a national securities exchange shall also file a duplicate original of such information, documents, and reports with the exchange.

(b) The Commission may prescribe, in regard to reports made pursuant to this title, the form or forms in which the required information shall be set forth, the items or details to be shown in the balance sheet and the earning statement, and the methods to be followed in the preparation of reports, in the appraisal or valuation of assets and liabilities, in the determination of depreciation and depletion, in the differentiation of recurring and nonrecurring income, in the differentiation of investment and operating income, and in the preparation, where the Commission deems it necessary or desirable, of separate and/or consolidated balance sheets or income accounts of any person directly or indirectly controlling or controlled by the issuer, or any person under direct or indirect common control with the issuer; but in the case of the reports of any person whose methods of accounting are prescribed under the provisions of any law of the United States, or any rule or regulation thereunder, the rules and regulations of the Commission with respect to reports shall not be inconsistent with the requirements imposed by such law or rule or regulation in respect of the same subject matter, (except that such rules and regulations of the Commission may be inconsistent with such requirements to the extent that the Commission determines that the public interest or the protection of investors so requires).

(2) Every issuer which has a class of securities registered pursuant to section 12 of this title and every issuer which is required to file reports pursuant to section 15(d) of this title shall—

(A) make and keep books, records, and accounts, which, in reasonable detail, accurately and fairly reflect the transactions and dispositions of the assets of the issuer; and

(B) devise and maintain a system of internal accounting controls sufficient to provide reasonable assurances that—

(i) transactions are executed in accordance with management's general or specific authorization;

(ii) transactions are recorded as necessary (I) to permit preparation of financial statements in conformity with generally accepted accounting principles or any other criteria applicable to such statements, and (II) to maintain accountability for assets;

(iii) access to assets is permitted only in accordance with management's general or specific authorization; and

(iv) the recorded accountability for assets is compared with the existing assets at reasonable intervals and appropriate action is taken with respect to any differences.

. . .

(c) If in the judgment of the Commission any report required under subsection (a) is inapplicable to any specified class or classes of issuers, the Commission shall require in lieu thereof the submission of such reports of comparable character as it may deem applicable to such class or classes of issuers.

(d)(1) Any person who, after acquiring directly or indirectly the beneficial ownership of any equity security of a class which is registered pursuant to section 12 of this title, or any equity security of an insurance company which would have been required to be so registered except for the exemption contained in section 12(g) (2) (G) of this title, or any equity security issued by a closed-end investment company registered under the Investment Company Act of 1940, is directly or indirectly the beneficial owner of more than 5 per centum of such class shall, within ten days after such acquisition, send to the issuer of the security at its principal executive office, by registered or certified mail, send to each exchange where the security is traded, and file with the Commission, a statement containing such of the following information, and such additional information, as the Commission may by rules and regulations prescribe as necessary or appropriate in the public interest or for the protection of investors—

(A) the background, and identity of, residence, and citizenship of, and the nature of such beneficial ownership by, such person and all other persons by whom or on whose behalf the purchases have been or are to be effected;

(B) the source and amount of the funds or other consideration used or to be used in making the purchases, and if any part of the purchase price or proposed purchase price is represented or is to be represented by funds or other consideration borrowed or otherwise obtained for the purpose of acquiring, holding, or trading such security, a description of the transaction and the names of the parties thereto, except that where a source of funds is a loan made in the ordinary course of business by a bank, as defined in section 3(a)(6) of this title, if the person filing such statement so requests, the name of the bank shall not be made available to the public;

(C) if the purpose of the purchases or prospective purchases is to acquire control of the business of the issuer of the securities, any plans or proposals which such persons may have to liquidate such issuer, to sell its assets to or merge it with any other persons, or to make any other major change in its business or corporate structure;

(D) the number of shares of such security which are beneficially owned, and the number of shares concerning which there is a right to acquire, directly or indirectly, by (i) such person, and (ii) by each associate of such person, giving the background, identity, residence and citizenship of each such associate; and

(E) information as to any contracts, arrangements, or understandings with any person with respect to any securities of the issuer, including but not limited to transfer of any of the securities, joint ventures, loan or option arrangements, puts or calls, guaranties of loans, guaranties against loss or guaranties of profits, division of losses or profits, or the giving or withholding of proxies, naming the persons with whom such contracts, arrangements, or understandings have been entered into, and giving the details thereof.

.   .   .

(3) When two or more persons act as a partnership, limited partnership, syndicate, or other group for the purpose of acquiring, holding, or disposing of securities of an issuer, such syndicate or group shall be deemed a "person" for the purposes of this subsection.   .   .

(e)(1) It shall be unlawful for an issuer which has a class of equity securities registered pursuant to section 12 of this title, or which is a closed-end investment company registered under the Investment Company Act of 1940, to purchase any equity security issued by it if such purchase is in contravention of such rules and regulations as the Commission, in the public interest or for the protection of investors, may adopt (A) to define acts and practices which are fraudulent, deceptive, or manipulative, and (B) to prescribe means reasonably designed to prevent such acts and practices. Such rules and regulations may require such issuer to provide holders of equity securities of such class with such information relating to the reasons for such purchase, the source of funds, the number of shares to be purchased, the price to be paid for such securities, the method of purchase, and such additional information, as the Commission deems necessary or appropriate in the public interest or for the protection of investors, or which the Commission deems to be material to a determination whether such security should be sold.

(e)(2) For the purpose of this subsection, a purchase by or for the issuer, or any person controlling, controlled by, or under the common control with the issuer, or a purchase subject to control of the issuer or any such person, shall be deemed to be a purchase by the issuer. The Commission shall have power to make rules and regulations implementing this paragraph in the public interest and for the protection of investors, including exemptive rules and regulations covering situations in which the Commission deems it unnecessary or inappropriate that a purchase of the type described in this paragraph shall be deemed to be a purchase by the issuer for purposes of some or all of the provisions of paragraph (1) of this subsection.

§ 14. PROXIES

(a) It shall be unlawful for any person, by the use of the mails or by any means or instrumentality of interstate commerce or of any facility of a national securities exchange or otherwise, in contravention of such rules and regulations as the Commission may prescribe as necessary or appropriate in the public interest or for the protection of investors, to solicit or to permit the use of his name to solicit any proxy or consent or authorization in respect of any security (other than an exempted security) registered pursuant to section 12 of this title.

(b) It shall be unlawful for any member of a national securities exchange, or any broker or dealer registered under this title, in contravention of such rules and regulations as the Commission may prescribe as necessary or appropriate in the public interest or for the protection of investors, to give, or to refrain from giving a proxy, consent, or authorization in respect of any security registered pursuant to section 12 of this title and carried for the account of a customer.

(c) Unless proxies, consents, or authorizations in respect of a security registered pursuant to section 12 of this title are solicited by or on behalf of the management of the issuer from the holders of record of such security in accordance with the rules and regulations prescribed under subsection (a) of this section, prior to any annual or other meeting of the holders of such security, such issuer shall, in accordance with rules and regulations prescribed by the Commission, file with the Commission and transmit to all holders of record of such security information substantially equivalent to the information which would be required to be transmitted if a solicitation were made. . . .

(d)(1) It shall be unlawful for any person, directly or indirectly, by use of the mails or by any means or instrumentality of interstate commerce or of any facility of a national securities exchange or otherwise, to make a tender offer for, or a request or invitation for tenders of, any class of any equity security which is registered pursuant to section 12 of this title, . . . if, after consummation thereof, such person would, directly or indirectly, be the beneficial owner of more than 5 per centum of such class, unless at the time copies of the offer or request or invitation are first published or sent or given to security holders such person has filed with the Commission a statement containing such of the information specified in section 13(d) of this title, and such additional information as the Commission may by rules and regulations prescribe as necessary or appropriate in the public interest or for the protection of investors. All requests or invitations for tenders or advertisements making a tender offer or requesting or inviting tenders of such a security shall be filed as a part of such statement and shall contain such of the information contained in such statement as the Commission may by rules and regulations prescribe. Copies of any additional material soliciting or requesting such tender offers subsequent to the initial solicitation or request shall contain such information as the Commission may by rules and regulations prescribe as necessary or appropriate in the public interest or for the protection of investors, and shall be filed with the Commission not later than the time copies of such material are first published or sent or given to security holders. Copies of all statements, in the form in which such material is furnished to security holders and the Commission, shall be sent to the issuer not later than the date such material is first published or sent or given to any security holders.

. . .

(2) When two or more persons act as a partnership, limited partnership, syndicate, or other group for the purpose of acquiring, holding, or disposing of securities of an issuer, such syndicate or group shall be deemed a "person" for purposes of this subsection.

(3) In determining, for purposes of this subsection, any percentage of a class of any security, such class shall be deemed to consist of the amount of the outstanding securities of such class, exclusive of any securities of such class held by or for the account of the issuer or a subsidiary of the issuer.

(4) Any solicitation or recommendation to the holders of such a security to accept or reject a tender offer or request or invitation for tenders shall be made in accordance with such rules and regulations as the Commission may prescribe as necessary or appropriate in the public interest or for the protection of investors.

(5) Securities deposited pursuant to a tender offer or request or invitation for tenders may be withdrawn by or on behalf of the depositor at any time until the expiration of seven days after the time definitive copies of the offer or request or invitation are first published or sent or given to security holders, and at any time after sixty days from the date of the original tender offer or request or invitation, except as the Commission may otherwise prescribe by rules, regulations, or order as necessary or appropriate in the public interest or for the protection of investors.

(6) Where any person makes a tender offer, or request or invitation for tenders, for less than all the outstanding equity securities of a class, and where a greater number of securities is deposited pursuant thereto within ten days after copies of the offer or request or invitation are first published or sent or given to security holders than such person is bound or willing to take up and pay for, the securities taken up shall be taken up as nearly as may be pro rata, disregarding fractions, according to the number of securities deposited by each depositor. The provisions of this subsection shall also apply to securities deposited within ten days after notice of an increase in the consideration offered to security holders, as described in paragraph (7), is first published or sent or given to security holders.

(7) Where any person varies the terms of a tender offer or request or invitation for tenders before the expiration thereof by increasing the consideration offered to holders of such securities, such person shall pay the

increased consideration to each security holder whose securities are taken up and paid for pursuant to the tender offer or request or invitation for tenders whether or not such securities have been taken up by such person before the variation of the tender offer or request or invitation.

. . .

(8) The provisions of this subsection shall not apply to any offer for, or request or invitation for tenders of, any security—

(A) if the acquisition of such security, together with all other acquisitions by the same person of securities of the same class during the preceding twelve months, would not exceed 2 per centum of that class;

` (B) by the issuer of such security; or

(C) which the Commission, by rules or regulations or by order, shall exempt from the provisions of this subsection as not entered into for the purpose of, and not having the effect of, changing or influencing the control of the issuer or otherwise as not comprehended within the purposes of this subsection.

(e) It shall be unlawful for any person to make any untrue statement of a material fact or omit to state any material fact necessary in order to make the statements made, in the light of the circumstances under which they are made, not misleading, or to engage in any fraudulent, deceptive, or manipulative acts or practices, in connection with any tender offer or request or invitation for tenders, or any solicitation of security holders in opposition to or in favor of any such offer, request, or invitation. The Commission shall, for the purposes of this subsection, by rules and regulations define, and prescribe means reasonably designed to prevent, such acts and practices as are fraudulent, deceptive, or manipulative.

(f) If, pursuant to any arrangement or understanding with the person or persons acquiring securities in a transaction subject to subsection (d) of this section or subsection (d) of section 13 of this title, any persons are to be elected or designated as directors of the issuer, otherwise than at a meeting of security holders, and the persons so elected or designated will constitute a majority of the directors of the issuer, then, prior to the time any such person takes office as a director, and in accordance with rules and regulations prescribed by the Commission, the issuer shall file with the Commission, and transmit to all holders of record of securities of the issuer who would be entitled to vote at a meeting for election of directors, information substantially equivalent to the information which would be required by subsection (a) or (c) of this section to be transmitted if such person or persons were nominees for election as directors at a meeting of such security holders.

§ 16. DIRECTORS, OFFICERS AND PRINCIPAL STOCKHOLDERS

(a) Every person who is directly or indirectly the beneficial owner of more than 10 per centum of any class of any equity security (other than an exempted security) which is registered pursuant to section 12 of this title, or who is a director or an officer of the issuer of such security, shall file, at the time of the registration of such security on a national securities exchange or by the effective date of a registration statement filed pursuant to section 12(g) of this title, or within ten days after he becomes such beneficial owner, director, or officer, a statement with the Commission (and, if such security is registered on a national securities exchange, also with the exchange) of the amount of all equity securities of such issuer of which he is the beneficial owner, and within ten days after the close of each calendar month thereafter, if there has been a change in such ownership during such month, shall file with the Commission (and if such security is registered on a national securities exchange, shall also file with the exchange), a statement indicating his ownership at the close of the calendar month and such changes in his ownership as have occurred during such calendar month.

(b) For the purpose of preventing the unfair use of information which may have been obtained by such beneficial owner, director, or officer by reason of his relationship to the issuer, any profit realized by him from any purchase and sale, or any sale and purchase, of any equity security of such issuer (other than an exempted security) within any period of less than six months, unless such security was acquired in good faith in connection with a debt previously contracted, shall inure to and be recoverable by the issuer, irrespective of any intention on the part of such beneficial owner, director, or officer in entering into such transaction of holding the security purchased or of not repurchasing the security sold for a period exceeding six months. Suit to recover such profit may be instituted at law or in equity in any court of competent jurisdiction by the issuer, or by the owner of any security of the issuer in the name and in behalf of the issuer if the issuer shall fail or refuse to bring such suit within sixty days after request or shall fail diligently to prosecute the same thereafter; but no such suit shall be brought more than two years after the date such profit was realized. This subsection shall not be construed to cover any transaction where such beneficial owner was not such both at the time of the purchase and sale, or the sale and purchase, of the security involved, or any transaction or transactions which the Commission by rules and regulations may exempt as not comprehended within the purpose of this subsection.

(c) It shall be unlawful for any such beneficial owner, director, or officer, directly or indirectly, to sell any equity security of such issuer (other than an exempted security), if the person selling the security or his principal (1) does not own the security sold, or (2) if owning the security, does not deliver it against such sale within twenty days thereafter, or does not within five days after such sale deposit it in the mails or other usual channels of transportation; but no person shall be deemed to have violated this subsection if he proves that notwithstanding the exercise of good faith he was unable to make such delivery or deposit within such time, or that to do so would cause undue inconvenience or expense.

(d) The provisions of subsection (b) of this section shall not apply to any purchase and sale, or sale and purchase, and the provisions of subsection (c) of this section shall not apply to any sale, of an equity security not then or theretofore held by him in an investment account, by a dealer in the ordinary course of his business and incident to the establishment or maintenance by him of a primary or secondary market (otherwise than on a national securities exchange or an exchange exempted from registration under section 5 of this title) for such security. The Commission may, by such rules and regulations as it deems necessary or appropriate in the public interest, define and prescribe terms and conditions with respect to securities held in an investment account and transactions made in the ordinary course of business and incident to the establishment or maintenance of a primary or secondary market.

(e) The provisions of this section shall not apply to foreign or domestic arbitrage transactions unless made in contravention of such rules and regulations as the Commission may adopt in order to carry out the purposes of this section.

§ 20. LIABILITIES OF CONTROLLING PERSONS

(a) Every person who, directly or indirectly, controls any person liable under any provision of this title or of any rule or regulation thereunder shall also be liable jointly and severally with and to the same extent as such controlled person to any person to whom such controlled person is liable, unless the controlling person acted in good faith and did not directly or indirectly induce the act or acts constituting the violation or cause of action.

(b) It shall be unlawful for any person, directly or indirectly, to do any act or thing which it would be unlawful for such person to do under the provisions of this title or any rule or regulation thereunder through or by means of any other person.

(c) It shall be unlawful for any director or officer of, or any owner of any securities issued by, any issuer required to file any document, report, or information under this title or any rule or regulation thereunder without just cause to hinder, delay, or obstruct the making or filing of any such document, report, or information.

§ 25. COURT REVIEW OF ORDERS AND RULES

(a)(1) A person aggrieved by a final order of the Commission entered pursuant to this title may obtain review of the order in the United States Court of Appeals for the circuit in which he resides or has his principal place of business, or for the District of Columbia Circuit, by filing in such court, within sixty days after the entry of the order, a written petition requesting that the order be modified or set aside in whole or in part.[7]

. . .

(b)(1) A person adversely affected by a rule of the Commission promulgated pursuant to Sections 6, 11, 11A, 15(c)(5) or (6), 15A, 17, 17A, or 19 of this title may obtain review of this rule in the United States Court of Appeals for the circuit in which he resides or has his principal place of business or for the District of Columbia Circuit, by filing in such court, within sixty days after the promulgation of the rule, a written petition requesting that the rule be set aside.

§ 27. JURISDICTION OF OFFENSES AND SUITS

The district courts of the United States, the United States District Court for the District of Columbia, and the United States courts of any Territory or other place subject to the jurisdiction of the United States shall have exclusive jurisdiction of violations of this title or the rules and regulations thereunder, and of all suits in equity and actions at law brought to enforce any liability or duty created by this title or the rules and regulations thereunder. Any criminal proceeding may be brought in the district wherein any act or transaction constituting the violation occurred. Any suit or action to enforce any liability or duty created by this title or rules and regulations thereunder, or to enjoin any violation of such title or rules and regulations, may be brought in any such district or in the district wherein the defendant is found or is an inhabitant or transacts business, and process in such cases may be served in any other district of which the defendant is an inhabitant or wherever the defendant may be found. . . .

§ 28. EFFECTS ON EXISTING LAW

(a) The rights and remedies provided by this title shall be in addition to any and all other rights and remedies that may exist at law or in equity; but no person permitted to maintain a suit for damages under the provisions of this title shall recover, through satisfaction of judgment in one or more actions, a total amount in excess of his actual damages on account of the act complained of. Nothing in this title shall affect the jurisdiction of the securities commission (or any agency or officer performing like functions) of any State over any security or any person insofar as it does not conflict with the provisions of this title or the rules and regulations thereunder.

. . .

§ 29. VALIDITY OF CONTRACTS

(a) Any condition, stipulation, or provision binding any person to waive compliance with any provision of this title or of any rule or regulation thereunder, or of any rule of an exchange required thereby shall be void.

---

7. At the time of the Medical Committee case, this subsection began: "Any person aggrieved by an order issued by the Commission in a proceeding under this title to which such person is a party may . . ."

(b) Every contract made in violation of any provision of this title or of any rule or regulation thereunder, and every contract (including any contract for listing a security on an exchange) heretofore or hereafter made the performance of which involves the violation of, or the continuance of any relationship or practice in violation of, any provision of this title or any rule or regulation thereunder, shall be void (1) as regards the rights of any person who, in violation of any such provision, rule, or regulation, shall have made or engaged in the performance of any such contract, and (2) as regards the rights of any person who, not being a party to such contract, shall have acquired any right thereunder with actual knowledge of the facts by reason of which the making or performance of such contract was in violation of any such provision, rule, or regulation: .   .   .

C. SELECTED SEC RULES AND REGULATIONS
RULE UNDER THE SECURITIES ACT OF 1933

Regulation D—Rules Governing the Limited Offer and Sale of Securities Without Registration Under the Securities Act of 1933 [8]

Preliminary Notes

1. The following rules relate to transactions exempted from the registration requirements of section 5 of the Securities Act of 1933 (the "Act") (15 U.S.C. 77a et seq., as amended). Such transactions are not exempt from the antifraud, civil liability, or other provisions of the federal securities laws. Issuers are reminded of their obligation to provide such further material information, if any, as may be necessary to make the information required under this regulation, in light of the circumstances under which it is furnished, not misleading.

2. Nothing in these rules obviates the need to comply with any applicable state law relating to the offer and sale of securities. Regulation D is intended to be a basic element in a uniform system of federal-state limited offering exemptions consistent with the provisions of sections 18 and 19(c) of the Act. In those states that have adopted Regulation D, or any version of Regulation D, special attention should be directed to the applicable state laws and regulations, including those relating to registration of person who receive remuneration in connection with the offer and sale of securities, to disqualification of issuers and other persons associated with offerings based on state administrative orders or judgments, and to requirements for filings of notices of sales.

3. Attempted compliance with any rule in Regulation D does not act as an exclusive election; the issuer can also claim the availability of any other applicable exemption. For instance, an issuer's failure to satisfy all the terms and conditions of Rule 506 shall not raise any presumption that the exemption provided by section 4(2) of the Act is not available.

4. These rules are available only to the issuer of the securities and not to any affiliate of that issuer or to any other person for resales of the issuer's securities. The rules provide an exemption only for the transactions

---

8. Regulation D was issued on March 16, 1982, and superseded Rules 146, 240 and 242. Its formal citation is 17 C.F.R. § 230.501 et seq.

in which the securities are offered or sold by the issuer, not for the securities themselves.

5. These rules may be used for business combinations that involve sales by virtue of rule 145(a)(17 CFR 230.145(a)) or otherwise.

6. In view of the objectives of these rules and the policies underlying the Act, regulation D is not available to any issuer for any transaction or chain of transactions that, although in technical compliance with these rules, is part of a plan or scheme to evade the registration provisions of the Act. In such cases, registration under the Act is required.

§ 230.501 Definitions and Terms Used in Regulation D.

As used in regulation D, the following terms shall have the meaning indicated:

(a) *Accredited Investor.* "Accredited investor" shall mean any person who comes within any of the following categories, or who the issuer reasonably believes comes within any of the following categories, at the time of the sale of the securities to that person:

(1) Any bank as defined in section 3(a)(2) of the Act whether acting in its individual or fiduciary capacity; insurance company as defined in section 2(13) of the Act; investment company registered under the Investment Company Act of 1940 or a business development company as defined in section 2(a)(48) of that Act; Small Business Investment Company licensed by the U. S. Small Business Administration under section 301(c) or (d) of the Small Business Investment Act of 1958; employee benefit plan within the meaning of Title I of the Employee Retirement Income Security Act of 1974, if the investment decision is made by a plan fiduciary, as defined in section 3(21) of such Act, which is either a bank, insurance company, or registered investment adviser, or if the employee benefit plan has total assets in excess of $5,000,000;

(2) Any private business development company as defined in section 202 (a)(22) of the Investment Advisers Act of 1940;

(3) Any organization described in Section 501(c)(3) of the Internal Revenue Code with total assets in excess of $5,000,000;

(4) Any director, executive officer, or general partner of the issuer of the securities being offered or sold, or any director, executive officer, or general partner of a general partner of that issuer;

(5) Any person who purchases at least $150,000 of the securities being offered, where the purchaser's total purchase price does not exceed 20 percent of the purchaser's net worth at the time of sale, or joint net worth with that person's spouse, for one or any combination of the following: (i) cash; (ii) securities for which market quotations are readily available, (iii) an unconditional obligation to pay cash or securities for which market quotations are readily available which obligation is to be discharged within five years of the sale of the securities to the purchaser, or (iv) the cancellation of any indebtedness owed by the issuer to the purchaser;

(6) Any natural person whose individual net worth, or joint net worth with that person's spouse, at the time of his purchase exceeds $1,000,000;

(7) Any natural person who had an individual income in excess of $200,000 in each of the two most recent years and who reasonably expects an income in excess of $200,000 in the current year; and

(8) Any entity in which all of the equity owners are accredited investors under paragraphs (a)(1), (2), (3), (4), (6), or (7) of this section.

(b) *Affiliate.* An "affiliate" of, or person "affiliated" with, a specified person shall mean a person that directly, or indirectly through one or more intermediaries, controls or is controlled by, or is under common control with, the person specified.

(c) *Aggregate Offering Price.* "Aggregate offering price" shall mean the sum of all cash, services, property, notes, cancellation of debt, or other consideration received by an issuer for issuance of its securities. . . .

(d) *Business Combination.* . . .

(e) *Calculation of Number of Purchasers.* For purposes of calculating the number of purchasers under §§ 230.505(b) and 230.506(b) only, the following shall apply:

(1) The following purchasers shall be excluded:

(i) Any relative, spouse or relative of the spouse of a purchaser who has the same principal residence as the purchaser;

(iii) Any trust or estate in which a purchaser and any of the persons related to him as specified in paragraph (e)(1)(i) or (e)(1)(iii) of this section collectively have more than 50 percent of the beneficial interest (excluding contingent interests);

(iii) Any corporation or other organization of which a purchaser and any of the persons related to him as specified in paragraph (e)(1)(i) or (e)(1)(ii) of this section collectively are beneficial owners of more than 50 percent of the equity securities (excluding directors' qualifying shares) or equity interests; and

(iv) Any accredited investor.

(2) A corporation, partnership or other entity shall be counted as one purchaser. . . .

(f) *Executive Officer.* "Executive officer" shall mean the president, any vice president in charge of a principal business unit, division or function (such as sales, administration or finance), any other officer who performs a policy making function, or any other person who performs similar policy making functions for the issuer. . . .

(g) *Issuer.* . . .

(h) *Purchaser Representative.* "Purchaser representative" shall mean any person who satisfies all of the following conditions or who the issuer reasonably believes satisfies all of the following conditions:

(1) Is not an affiliate, director, officer or other employee of the issuer, or beneficial owner of 10 percent or more of any class of the equity securities or 10 percent or more of the equity interest in the issuer, except where the purchaser is:

(i) A relative of the purchaser representative by blood, marriage or adoption and not more remote than a first cousin;

(ii) A trust or estate in which the purchaser representative and any persons related to him as specified in paragraph (h)(1)(i) or (h)(1)(iii) of this section collectively have more than 50 percent of the beneficial interest excluding contingent interest) or of which the purchaser representative serves as trustee, executor, or in any similar capacity; or

(iii) A corporation or other organization of which the purchaser representative and any persons related to him as specified in paragraph (h)(1)(i) or (h)(1)(ii) of this section collectively are the beneficial owners of more than 50 percent of the equity securities excluding directors' qualifying shares) or equity interests;

(2) Has such knowledge and experience in financial and business matters that he is capable of evaluating, alone, or together with other purchaser representatives of the purchaser, or together with the purchaser, the merits and risks of the prospective investment;

(3) Is acknowledged by the purchaser in writing, during the course of the transaction, to be his purchaser representative in connection with evaluating the merits and risks of the prospective investment; and

(4) Discloses to the purchaser in writing prior to the acknowledgment specified in paragraph (h)(3) of this section any material relationship between himself or his affiliates and the issuer or its affiliates that then exists, that is mutually understood to be contemplated, or that has existed at any time during the previous two years, and any compensation received or to be received as a result of such relationship.

§ 230.502   General conditions to be met.

The following conditions shall be applicable to offers and sales made under regulation D:

(a) *Integration.* All sales that are part of the same regulation D offering must meet all of the terms and conditions of regulation D. Offers and sales that are made more than six months before the start of a regulation D offering or are made more than six months after completion of a regulation D offering will not be considered part of that regulation D offering, so long as during those six month periods there are no offers or sales of securities by or for the issuer that are of the same or a similar class as those offered or sold under regulation D, other than those offers or sales of securities under an employee benefit plan as defined in rule 405 under the Act.

(b) *Information Requirements.*—(1) *When Information Must Be Furnished.*

(i) If the issuer sells securities either under § 230.504 or only to accredited investors, paragraph (b) of this § 230.502 does not require that specific information be furnished to purchasers.

(ii) If the issuer sells securities under § 230.505 or 230.506 to any purchaser that is not an accredited investor, the issuer shall furnish the information specified in paragraph (b)(2) of this section to all purchasers during the course of the offering and prior to sale.

(2) *Type of Information to Be Furnished.* (i) If the issuer is not subject to the reporting requirements of section 13 or 15(d) of the Exchange Act, the issuer shall furnish the following information, to the extent material to an understanding of the issuer, its business, and the securities being offered:

(A) *Offerings up to $5,000,000.* The same kind of information as would be required in Part I of Form S–18, except that only the financial statements for the issuer's most recent fiscal year must be certified by an independent public or certified accountant. If Form S–18 is not available to an issuer. then the issuer shall furnish the same kind of information as would be required in Part I of a registration statement filed under the Act on the form that the issuer would be entitled to use, except that only the financial statements for the most recent two fiscal years prepared in accordance with generally accepted accounting principles shall be furnished and only the financial statements for the issuer's most recent fiscal year shall be certified by an independent public or certified accountant. If an issuer, other than a limited partnership, cannot obtain audited financial statements without unreasonable effort or expense, then only the issuer's balance sheet, which shall be dated within 120 days of the start of the offering, must be audited. If the issuer is a limited partnership and cannot obtain the required financial statements without unreasonable effort or expense, it may furnish financial statements that have been prepared on the basis of federal income tax requirements and examined and reported on in accordance with generally accepted auditing standards by an independent public or certified accountant.

(B) *Offerings Over $5,000,000.* The same kind of information as would be required in Part I of a registration statement filed under the Act on the form that the issuer would be entitled to use. If an issuer, other than a limited partnership, cannot obtain audited financial statements without unreasonable effort or expense, then only the issuer's balance sheet, which shall be dated within 120 days of the start of the offering, must be audited. If the issuer is a limited partnership and cannot obtain the required financial statements without unreasonable effort or expense, it may furnish financial statements that have been prepared on the basis of federal income tax requirements and examined and reported on in accordance with generally accepted auditing standards by an independent public or certified accountant.

(ii) If the issuer is subject to the reporting requirements of section 13 or 15(d) of the Exchange Act, the issuer shall furnish the information specified in paragraph (b)(2)(ii)(A) or (b)(2)(ii)(B) of this section, and in either event the information specified in paragraph (b)(2)(ii)(C) of this section:

(A) The issuer's annual report to shareholders for the most recent fiscal year, if such annual report meets the requirements of § 240.14a–3 or 240.14c–3 under the Exchange Act, the definitive proxy statement filed in connection with that annual report, and, if requested by the purchaser in writing, a copy of the issuer's most recent Form 10–K under the Exchange Act.

(B) The information contained in an annual report on Form 10–K under the Exchange Act or in a registration statement on Form S–1 under the Act or on Form 10 (17 CFR 249.210) under the Exchange Act, whichever filing is the most recent required to be filed.

(C) The information contained in any reports or documents required to be filed by the issuer under sections 13(a), 14(a), 14(c), and 15(d) of the Exchange Act since the distribution or filing of the report or registration statement specified in paragraph (A) or (B), and a brief description of the securities being offered, the use of the proceeds from the offering, and any material changes in the issuer's affairs that are not disclosed in the documents furnished.

(iii) Exhibits required to be filed with the Commission as part of a registration statement or report, other than an annual report to shareholders or parts of that report incorporated by reference in a Form 10–K report, need not be furnished to each purchaser if the contents of the exhibits are identified and the exhibits are made available to the purchaser, upon his written request, prior to his purchase.

(iv) At a reasonable time prior to the purchase of securities by any purchaser that is not an accredited investor in a transaction under § 230.505 or 230.506, the issuer shall furnish the purchaser a brief description in writing of any written information concerning the offering that has been provided by the issuer to any accredited investor. The issuer shall furnish any portion or all of this information to the purchaser, upon his written request, prior to his purchase.

(v) The issuer shall also make available to each purchaser at a reasonable time prior to his purchase of securities in a transaction under § 230.505 or 230.506 the opportunity to ask questions and receive answers concerning the terms and conditions of the offering and to obtain any additional information which the issuer possesses or can acquire without unreasonable effort or expense that is necessary to verify the accuracy of information furnished under paragraph (b)(2)(i) or (ii) of this section.

. . .

(c) *Limitation on Manner of Offering.* Except as provided in § 230.504 (b)(1), neither the issuer nor any person acting on its behalf shall offer or sell the securities by any form of general solicitation or general advertising, including, but not limited to, the following:

(1) Any advertisement, article, notice or other communication published in any newspaper, magazine, or similar media or broadcast over television or radio; and

(2) Any seminar or meeting whose attendees have been invited by any general solicitation or general advertising.

(d) *Limitations on Resale.* Except as provided in § 230.504(b)(1), securities acquired in a transaction under regulation D shall have the status of securities acquired in a transaction under section 4(2) of the Act, and cannot be resold without registration under the Act or an exemption therefrom. The issuer shall exercise reasonable care to assure that the purchasers of the securities are not underwriters within the meaning of section 2(11) of the Act, which reasonable care shall include, but not be limited to, the following:

(1) Reasonable inquiry to determine if the purchaser is acquiring the securities for himself or for other persons;

(2) Written disclosure to each purchaser prior to sale that the securities have not been registered under the Act and, therefore, cannot be resold unless they are registered under the Act or unless an exemption from registration is available; and

(3) Placement of a legend on the certificate or other document that evidences the securities stating that the securities have not been registered under the Act and setting forth or referring to the restrictions on transferability and sale of the securities.

§ 230.503   Filing of Notice of Sales.

[Rules as to the number of copies required and the forms, signatures and times specified are omitted]

§ 230.504   Exemption for limited offers and sales of securities not exceeding $500,000.

(a) *Exemption.* Offers and sales of securities that satisfy the conditions in paragraph (b) of this Section by an issuer that is not subject to the reporting requirements of section 13 or 15(d) of the Exchange Act and that is not an investment company shall be exempt from the provisions of section 5 of the Act under section 3(b) of the Act.

(b) *Conditions to Be Met.*—(1) *General Conditions.* To qualify for exemption under this Section offers and sales must satisfy the terms and conditions of §§ 230.501 through 230.503, except that the provisions of §§ 230.-502(c) and (d) shall not apply to offers and sales of securities under this Section that are made exclusively in one or more states each of which provides for the registration of the securities and requires the delivery of a disclosure document before sale and that are made in accordance with those state provisions.

(2) *Specific Condition.*—(i) *Limitation on Aggregate Offering Price.* The aggregate offering price for an offering of securities under this § 230.-504, as defined in § 230.501(c), shall not exceed $500,000 less the aggregate offering price for all securities sold within the twelve months before the start of and during the offering of securities under this Section in reliance on any exemption under Section 3(b) of the Act or in violation of Section 5(a) of the Act.

§ 230.505   Exemptions for limited offers and sales of securities not exceeding $5,000,000.

(a) *Exemption.* Offers and sales of securities that satisfy the conditions in paragraph (b) of this section by an issuer that is not an investment company shall be exempt from the provisions of section 5 of the Act under section 3(b) of the Act.

(b) *Conditions to Be Met.*—(1) *General Conditions.* To qualify for exemption under this section, offers and sales must satisfy the terms and conditions of §§ 230.501 through 230.503.

(2) *Specific Conditions.*—(i) *Limitation on Aggregate Offering Price.* The aggregate offering price for an offering of securities under this § 230.-505, as defined in § 203.501(c), shall not exceed $5,000,000, less the aggregate offering price for all securities sold within the twelve months before the start of and during the offering of securities under this section in reliance on any exemption under section 3(b) of the Act or in violation of section 5(a) of the Act.

(ii) *Limitation on Number of Purchasers.* The issuer shall reasonably believe that there are no more than 35 purchasers of securities from the issuer in any offering under this section.

(iii) *Disqualifications.* No exemption under this § 230.505 shall be available for the securities of any issuer described in § 230.252(c), (d), (e), or (f) of regulation A, except that for purposes of this section only:

(A) The term "filing of the notification required by § 230.255" as used in § 230.252(c), (d), (e) and (f) shall mean the first sale of securities under this section;

(B) The term "underwriter" as used in § 230.252(d) and (e) shall mean a person that has been or will be paid directly or indirectly remuneration for solicitation of purchasers in connection with sales of securities under this § 230.505; and

(C) Paragraph (b)(2)(iii) of this section shall not apply to any issuer if the Commission determines, upon a showing of good cause, that it is not necessary under the circumstances that the exemption be denied. Any such determination shall be without prejudice to any other action by the Commission in any other proceeding or matter with respect to the issuer or any other person.

(ii) *Nature of Purchasers.* The issuer shall reasonably believe immediately prior to making any sale that each purchaser who is not an accredited investor either alone or with his purchaser representative(s) has such knowledge and experience in financial and business matters that he is capable of evaluating the merits and risks of the prospective investment.

§ 230.506 **Exemption for Limited Offers and Sales Without Regard to Dollar Amount of Offering.**

(a) *Exemption.* Offers and sales of securities by an issuer that satisfy the conditions in paragraph (b) of this section shall be deemed to be transactions not involving any public offering within the meaning of section 4(2) of the Act.

(b) *Conditions to Be Met.*—(1) *General Conditions.* To qualify for exemption under this section, offers and sales must satisfy all the terms and conditions of §§ 230.501 through 230.503.

(2) *Specific Conditions.*—(i) *Limitation on Number of Purchasers.* The issuer shall reasonably believe that there are no more than 35 purchasers of securities from the issuer in any offering under this section.

(ii) *Nature of Purchasers.* The issuer shall reasonably believe immediately prior to making any sale that each purchaser who is not an accredited investor either alone or with his purchaser representative(s) has such knowledge and experience in financial and business matters that he is capable of evaluating the merits and risks of the prospective investment.

RULES UNDER THE SECURITIES
EXCHANGE ACT OF 1934 [9]

Rule 10b–5. Employment of Manipulative and Deceptive Devices

It shall be unlawful for any person, directly or indirectly, by the use of any means or instrumentality of interstate commerce, or of the mails, or of any facility of any national securities exchange,

(a) to employ any device, scheme, or artifice to defraud,

(b) to make any untrue statement of a material fact or to omit to state a material fact necessary in order to make the statements made,

---

9. The formal citation to these rules is to 17 C.F.R. Sec. 240.

in the light of the circumstances under which they were made, not misleading, or

(c) to engage in any act, practice, or course of business which operates or would operate as a fraud or deceit upon any person, in connection with the purchase or sale of any security.

Rule 14a–2.   Solicitations to Which Rules Apply

Sections 240.14a–3 to 240.14a–121 apply to every solicitation [10] of a proxy with respect to securities registered pursuant to Section 12 of the Act, whether or not trading in such securities has been suspended, except that:

(a) Sections 240.14a–3 to 240.14a–12 do not apply to the following:

(1) Any solicitation by a person in respect to securities carried in his name or in the name of his nominee (otherwise than as voting trustee) or held in his custody, if such person—

(i) Receives no commission or remuneration for such solicitation, directly or indirectly, other than reimbursement of reasonable expenses.

(ii) Furnishes promptly to the person solicited a copy of all soliciting material with respect to the same subject matter or meeting received from all persons who shall furnish copies thereof for such purpose and who shall, if requested, defray the reasonable expenses to be incurred in forwarding such material, and

(iii) In addition, does no more than impartially instruct the person solicited to forward a proxy to the person, if any, to whom the person solicited desires to give a proxy, or impartially request from the person solicited instructions as to the authority to be conferred by the proxy and state that a proxy will be given if no instructions are received by a certain date.

(2) Any solicitation by a person in respect of securities of which he is the beneficial owner;

(3) Any solicitation involved in the offer and sale of securities registered under the Securities Act of 1933;

(6) Any solicitation through the medium of a newspaper advertisement which informs security holders of a source from which they may obtain copies of a proxy statement, form of proxy and any other soliciting material and does no more than (i) name the issuer, (ii) state the reason for the advertisement, and (iii) identify the proposal or proposals to be acted upon by security holders.

(b) Securities 240.14a–3 to 240.14a–8 and 240.14a–10 to 240.14a–12 do not apply to the following:

(1) Any solicitation made otherwise than on behalf of the issuer where the total number of persons solicited is not more than ten; and

(2) The furnishing of proxy voting advice by any person (the "advisor") to any other person with whom the advisor has a business relationship, if:

---

10. Rule 14a–1(f) defines a "solicitation" to include a request for a proxy, a request to execute, not to execute or to revoke a proxy or communications calculated to have such consequences. It excludes furnishing proxy forms at the security holder's request, acts required by Rule 14a–7 or performing ministerial acts on behalf of the solicitor.

(i) The advisor renders financial advice in the ordinary course of his business;

(ii) The advisor discloses to the recipient of the advice any significant relationship with the issuer or any of its affiliates, or a shareholder proponent of the matter on which advice is given, as well as any material interest of the advisor in such matter;

(iii) The advisor receives no special commission or remuneration for furnishing the proxy voting advice from any person other than a recipient of the advice and other persons who receive similar advice under this subsection; and

(iv) The proxy voting advice is not furnished on behalf of any person soliciting proxies or on behalf of a participant in an election subject to the provisions of Rule 14a–11.

Rule 14a–3. Information to be Furnished to Security Holders

(a) No solicitation subject to this regulation shall be made unless each person solicited is concurrently furnished or has previously been furnished with a written proxy statement containing the information specified in Schedule 14A . . .

(b) If the solicitation is made on behalf of the issuer, and relates to an annual meeting of security holders at which directors are to be elected, each proxy statement furnished pursuant to paragraph (a) shall be accompanied or preceded by an annual report to security holders as follows:

(1) The report shall include, for the registrant and its subsidiaries consolidated, audited balance sheets as of the end of the two most recent fiscal years and audited statements of income and changes in financial position for each of the three most recent fiscal years prepared in accordance with Regulation S–X . . .

. . .

(5)(i) The report shall contain the selected financial data required by Item 301 of Regulation S–K . . .

(ii) The report shall contain management's discussion and analysis of financial condition and results of operations required by Item 303 of Regulation S–K . . .

(6) The report shall contain a brief description of the business done by the issuer and its subsidiaries during the most recent fiscal year which will, in the opinion of management, indicate the general nature and scope of the business of the issuer and its subsidiaries.

(7) The report shall contain information relating to the issuer's industry segments, classes of similar products or services, foreign and domestic operations and export sales . . .

(8) The report shall identify each of the issuer's directors and executive officers, and shall indicate the principal occupation or employment of each such person and the name and principal business of any organization by which such person is employed.

. . .

(10) Management's proxy statement, or the report, shall contain an undertaking in bold face or otherwise reasonably prominent type to provide without charge to each person solicited, on the written request of any such

person, a copy of the issuer's annual report on Form 10–K including the financial statements and the financial statement schedules, required to be filed with the Commission pursuant to Rule 13a–1 under the Act for the issuer's most recent fiscal year, and shall indicate the name and address of the person to whom such a written request is to be directed. . . .

(11) Subject to the foregoing requirements, the report may be in any form deemed suitable by management and the information required by paragraphs (b)(5) to (b)(10) of this section may be presented in an appendix or other separate section of the report, provided that the attention of security holders is called to such presentation.

Rule 14a–4. Requirements as to Proxy

(a) The form of proxy (1) shall indicate in bold-face type whether or not the proxy is solicited on behalf of the issuer's board of directors or, if provided other than by a majority of the board of directors, shall indicate in bold-face type on whose behalf the solicitation is made; (2) shall provide a specifically designated blank space for dating the proxy and (3) shall identify clearly and impartially each matter or group of related matters intended to be acted upon, whether proposed by the issuer or by security holders. No reference need be made, however, to proposals as to which discretionary authority is conferred pursuant to paragraph (c).

(b)(1) Means shall be provided in the form of proxy whereby the person solicited is afforded an opportunity to specify by boxes a choice between approval or disapproval of each matter or group of related matters referred to therein as intended to be acted upon, other than elections to office. A proxy may confer discretionary authority with respect to matters as to which a choice is not so specified provided the form of proxy states in bold-face type how it is intended to vote the shares represented by the proxy in each such case.

(2) A form of proxy which provides for the election of directors shall set forth the names of persons nominated for election as directors. Such form of proxy shall clearly provide any of the following means for security holders to withhold authority to vote for each nominee:

(i) A box opposite the name of each nominee which may be marked to indicate that authority to vote for such nominee is withheld; or

(ii) An instruction in bold-face type which indicates that the security holder may withhold authority to vote for any nominee by lining through or otherwise striking out the name of any nominee; or

(iii) Designated blank spaces in which the shareholder may enter the names of nominees with respect to whom the shareholder chooses to withhold authority to vote; or

(iv) Any other similar means, provided that clear instructions are furnished indicating how the shareholder may withhold authority to vote for any nominee.

Such form of proxy also may provide a means for the security holder to grant authority to vote for the nominees set forth, as a group, provided that there is a similar means for the security holder to withhold authority to vote for such group of nominees. Any such form of proxy which is executed by the security holder in such manner as not to withhold authority to vote for the election of any nominee shall be deemed to grant such authority, provided that the form of proxy so states in bold-face type.

(c) A proxy may confer discretionary authority to vote with respect to any of the following matters:

(1) Matters which the persons making the solicitation do not know, a reasonable time before the solicitation, are to be presented at the meeting, if a specific statement to that effect is made in the proxy statement or form of proxy;

(2) Approval of the minutes of the prior meeting if such approval does not amount to ratification of the action taken at that meeting;

(3) The election of any person to any office for which a bona fide nominee is named in the proxy statement and such nominee is unable to serve or for good cause will not serve;

(4) Any proposal omitted from the proxy statement and form of proxy pursuant to Rule 14a–8 or 14a–9;

(5) Matters incident to the conduct of the meeting.

(d) No proxy shall confer authority (1) to vote for the election of any person to any office for which a bona fide nominee is not named in the proxy statement, or (2) to vote at any annual meeting other than the next annual meeting (or any adjournment thereof) to be held after the date on which the proxy statement and form of proxy are first sent or given to security holders. A person shall not be deemed to be a bona fide nominee and he shall not be named as such unless he has consented to being named in the proxy statement and to serve if elected.

(e) The proxy statement or form of proxy shall provide, subject to reasonable specified conditions, that the shares represented by the proxy will be voted and that where the person solicited specifies by means of a ballot provided pursuant to paragraph (b) a choice with respect to any matter to be acted upon, the shares will be voted in accordance with the specifications so made.

Rule 14a–5. Presentation of Information in Proxy Statement

(a) The information included in the proxy statement shall be clearly presented and the statements made shall be divided into groups according to subject matter and the various groups of statements shall be preceded by appropriate headings. The order of items and sub-items in the schedule need not be followed. Where practicable and appropriate, the information shall be presented in tabular form. All amounts shall be stated in figures. Information required by more than one applicable item need not be repeated. No statement need be made in response to any item or sub-item which is inapplicable.

(b) Any information required to be included in the proxy statement as to terms of securities or other subject matter which from a standpoint of practical necessity must be determined in the future may be stated in terms of present knowledge and intention. To the extent practicable, the authority to be conferred concerning each such matter shall be confined within limits reasonably related to the need for discretionary authority. Subject to the foregoing, information which is not known to the persons on whose behalf the solicitation is to be made and which it is not reasonably within the power of such persons to ascertain or procure may be omitted, if a brief statement of the circumstances rendering such information unavailable is made.   .   .   .

Rule 14a–6.   Material Required to be Filed

(a) Five preliminary copies of the proxy statement and form of proxy and any other soliciting material to be furnished to security holders concurrently therewith shall be filed with the Commission at least 10 days prior to the date definitive copies of such material are first sent or given to security holders, or such shorter period prior to that date as the Commission may authorize upon a showing of good cause therefor. In computing the 10-day period the filing date of the preliminary material is to be counted as the first day and the eleventh day is the date on which definitive material may be mailed to security holders.

> *Note.* The officials responsible for the preparation of the preliminary material should make every effort to verify the accuracy and completeness of the information required by the applicable rules. The preliminary material should be filed with the Commission at the earliest practicable date. It should be accompanied by a letter, over the signature of an officer of the company or its counsel, stating whether the current preliminary material merely reflects an updating of the prior year's material (e. g., changes in the board of directors or nominees for election to the board) or includes changes of a material nature. All changes from the previously filed material should be identified in an accompanying marked copy of the proxy statement. If a change is material, the letter should include any explanatory comment which may be of assistance in the expeditious processing of the material.

(b) Five preliminary copies of any additional soliciting material, relating to the same meeting or subject matter, furnished to security holders subsequent to the proxy statement shall be filed with the Commission at least two days (exclusive of Saturdays, Sundays or holidays) prior to the date copies of such material are first sent or given to security holders, or such shorter period prior to such date as the Commission may authorize upon a showing of good cause therefor.   .   .   .

Rule 14a–7.   Mailing Communications for Security Holders

If the issuer has made or intends to make any solicitation subject to this regulation, the issuer shall perform such of the following acts as may be duly requested in writing with respect to the same subject matter or meeting by any security holder who is entitled to vote on such matter or to vote at such meeting and who shall defray the reasonable expenses to be incurred by the issuer in the performance of the act or acts requested.

(a) The issuer shall mail or otherwise furnish to such security holder the following information as promptly as practicable after the receipt of such request:

(1) A statement of the approximate number of holders of record of any class of securities, any of the holders of which have been or are to be solicited on behalf of the issuer, or any group of such holders which the security holder shall designate.

(2) If the issuer has made or intends to make, through bankers, brokers or other persons any solicitation of the beneficial owners of securities of any class, a statement of the approximate number of such beneficial owners, or any group of such owners which the security holder shall designate.

(3) An estimate of the cost of mailing a specified proxy statement, form of proxy or other communication to such holders, including insofar as known or reasonably available, the estimated handling and mailing costs of the bankers, brokers or other persons specified in (2) above.

(b) (1) Copies of any proxy statement, form of proxy or other communication furnished by the security holder shall be mailed by the issuer to such of the holders of record specified in (a) (1) above as the security holder shall designate. The issuer shall also mail to each banker, broker, or other persons specified in (a) (2) above a sufficient number of copies of such proxy statement, form of proxy or other communication as will enable the banker, broker, or other person to furnish a copy thereof to each beneficial owner solicited or to be solicited through him.

(2) Any such material which is furnished by the security holder shall be mailed with reasonable promptness by the issuer after receipt of a tender of the material to be mailed, of envelopes or other containers therefor and of postage or payment for postage.   .   .   .

(3) The issuer shall not be responsible for such proxy statement, form of proxy or other communication.

(c) In lieu of performing the acts specified above, the issuer may, at its option, furnish promptly to such security holder a reasonably current list of the names and addresses of such of the holders of record specified in (a) (1) above as the security holder shall designate, and a list of the names and addresses of such of the bankers, brokers or other persons specified in (a) (2) above as the security holder shall designate together with a statement of the approximate number of beneficial owners solicited or to be solicited through each such banker, broker or other person and a schedule of the handling and mailing costs of each such banker, broker or other person if such schedule has been supplied to the issuer.

.   .   .

Rule 14a–8. Proposals of Security Holders

(a) If any security holder of an issuer notifies issuer of his intention to present a proposal for action at a forthcoming meeting of the issuer's security holders, the issuer shall set forth the proposal in its proxy statement and identify it in its form of proxy and provide means by which security holders can make the specification required by Rule 14a–4(b). Notwithstanding the foregoing, the issuer shall not be required to include the proposal in its proxy statement or form of proxy unless the security holder (hereinafter, the "proponent") has complied with the requirements of this paragraph and paragraphs (b) and (c) hereof:

(1) *Eligibility.* At the time he submits the proposal, the proponent shall be a record or beneficial owner of a security entitled to be voted at the meeting on his proposal, and he shall continue to own such security through the date on which the meeting is held. If the issuer requests documentary support for a proponent's claim that he is a beneficial owner of a voting security of the issuer, the proponent shall furnish appropriate documentation within 10 business days after receiving the request. In the event the issuer includes the proponent's proposal in its proxy soliciting materials for the meeting and the proponent fails to comply with the requirement that he continuously be a voting security holder through the meeting date, the issuer shall not be required to include any proposals submitted by the proponent in its proxy soliciting materials for any meeting held in the following two calendar years.

(2) *Notice.* The proponent shall notify the issuer in writing of his intention to appear personally at the meeting to present his proposal for action. The proponent shall furnish the requisite notice at the time he submits the proposal, except that if he was unaware of the notice requirement at that time, he shall comply with it within 10 business days after being informed of it by the issuer. If the proponent, after furnishing in good faith the notice required by this provision, subsequently determines that he will be unable to appear personally at the meeting, he shall arrange to have another security holder of the issuer present his proposal on his behalf at the meeting. In the event the proponent of his proxy fails, without good cause, to present the proposal for action at the meeting, the issuer shall not be required to include any proposals submitted by the proponent in its proxy soliciting materials for any meeting held in the following two calendar years.

(3) *Timeliness.* The proponent shall submit his proposal sufficiently far in advance of the meeting so that it is received by the issuer within the following time periods:

(i) *Annual Meetings.* A proposal to be presented at an annual meeting shall be received at the issuer's principal executive offices not less than 90 days in advance of the date of the issuer's proxy statement released to security holders in connection with the previous year's annual meeting of security holders, except that if no annual meeting was held in the previous year or the date of the annual meeting has been changed by more than 30 calendar days from the date of the previous year's annual meeting a proposal shall be received by the issuer a reasonable time before the solicitation is made.

(ii) *Other Meetings.* A proposal to be presented at any meeting other than an annual meeting shall be received a reasonable time before the solicitation is made.

Note: In order to curtail controversy as to the date on which a proposal was received by the management, it is suggested that proponents submit their proposals by Certified Mail-Return Receipt Requested.

(4) *Number and Length of Proposals.* The proponent may submit a maximum of two proposals of not more than 300 words each for inclusion in the management's proxy materials for a meeting of security holders. If the proponent fails to comply with either of these requirements, or if he fails to comply with the 200-word limit on supporting statements mentioned in paragraph (b), he shall be provided the opportunity by the issuer to reduce, within 10 business days, the items submitted by him to the limits required by this rule.

(b) If the issuer opposes any proposal received from a proponent, it shall also, at the request of the proponent, include in its proxy statement a statement of the proponent of not more than 200 words [11] in support of the proposal, which statement shall not include the name and address of the proponent. The statement and request of the proponent shall be furnished to the issuer at the time that the proposal is furnished and the issuer shall not be responsible for such statement. The proxy statement shall also include either the name and address of the proponent or a statement that such information will be furnished by the issuer or by the Commission to any person, orally or in writing as requested, promptly upon the receipt of any oral or written request therefor. If the name and address of the proponent are omitted from the proxy statement, they shall be furnished to the Commission at the time of filing the issuer's preliminary proxy material pursuant to Rule 14a–6(a).

(c) The issuer may omit a proposal and any statement in support thereof from its proxy statement and form of proxy under any of the following circumstances [12]:

(1) If the proposal is, under the laws of the issuer's domicile, not a proper subject for action by security holders.

Note: A proposal that may be improper under the applicable state law when framed as a mandate or directive may be proper when framed as a recommendation or request.

(2) If the proposal would, if implemented, require the issuer to violate any state law or federal law of the United States, or any law of any foreign jurisdiction, to which the issuer is subject, except that this provision shall not apply with respect to any foreign law compliance with which would be violative of any state law or federal law of the United States;

(3) If the proposal or the supporting statement is contrary to any of the Commission's proxy rules and regulations, including Rule 14a–9, which prohibits false or misleading statements in proxy soliciting materials;

---

11. At the time of the Medical Committee case the security holder's statement was limited to 100 words.

12. At the time of the Medical Committee case the exclusions in subparagraph (c) were appreciably different. In particular, the court refers to the following exclusion:

(2) If it clearly appears that the proposal is submitted by the security holder primarily for the purpose of enforcing a personal claim or redressing a personal grievance against the issuer or its management, or primarily for the purpose of promoting general economic, political, racial, religious, social or similar causes;

. . . .

(4) If the proposal relates to the enforcement of a personal claim or the redress of a personal grievance against the issuer, its management, or any other person;

(5) If the proposal deals with a matter that is not significantly related to the issuer's business;

(6) If the proposal deals with a matter that is beyond the issuer's power to effectuate;

(7) If the proposal deals with a matter relating to the conduct of the ordinary business operations of the issuer;

(8) If the proposal relates to an election to office;

(9) If the proposal is counter to a proposal to be submitted by the issuer at the meeting;

(10) If the proposal has been rendered moot;

(11) If the proposal is substantially duplicative of a proposal previously submitted to the issuer by another proponent, which proposal will be included in the issuer's proxy material for the meeting;

(12) If substantially the same proposal has previously been submitted to security holders in the issuer's proxy statement and form of proxy relating to any annual or special meeting of security holders held within the preceding 5 calendar years, it may be omitted from the issuer's proxy materials relating to any meeting of security holders held within 3 calendar years after the latest such previous submission:

Provided, That—

(i) If the proposal was submitted at only one meeting during such preceding period, it received less than 3 percent of the total number of votes cast in regard thereto; or

(ii) If the proposal was submitted at only two meetings during such preceding period, it received at the time of its second submission less than 6 percent of the total number of votes cast in regard thereto; or

(iii) If the prior proposal was submitted at three or more meetings during such preceding period, it received at the time of its latest submission less than 10 percent of the total number of votes cast in regard thereto; and

(13) If the proposal relates to specific amounts of cash or stock dividends.

(d) Whenever the issuer asserts, for any reason, that a proposal and any statement in support thereof received from a proponent may properly be omitted from its proxy statement and form of proxy, it shall file with the Commission, not later than 50 days prior to the date the preliminary copies of the proxy statement and form of proxy are filed pursuant to Rule 14a–6(a), or such shorter period prior to such date as the Commission or its staff may permit, five copies of the following items: (1) the proposal; (2) any statement in support thereof as received from the proponent; (3) a statement of the reasons why the issuer deems such omission to be proper in the particular case; and (4) where such reasons are based on matters of law, a supporting opinion of counsel. The issuer shall at the same time, if it has not already done so, notify the proponent of its intention to omit the proposal from its proxy statement and form of proxy and shall forward to him a copy of the statement of reasons why the issuer deems the omission of the proposal to be proper and a copy of such supporting opinion of counsel.

. . .

Rule 14a–9. False or Misleading Statements

(a) No solicitation subject to this regulation shall be made by means of any proxy statement, form of proxy, notice of meeting or other communication, written or oral, containing any statement which, at the time and in the light of the circumstances under which it is made, is false or misleading with respect to any material fact, or which omits to state any material fact necessary in order to make the statements therein not false or misleading or necessary to correct any statement in any earlier communication with respect to the solicitation of a proxy for the same meeting or subject matter which has become false or misleading.

(b) The fact that a proxy statement, form of proxy or other soliciting material has been filed with or examined by the Commission shall not be deemed a finding by the Commission that such material is accurate or complete or not false or misleading, or that the Commission has passed upon the merits of or approved any statement contained therein or any matter to be acted upon by security holders. No representation contrary to the foregoing shall be made.

Note: The following are some examples of what, depending upon particular facts and circumstances, may be misleading within the meaning of this rule:

(a) Predictions as to specific future market values.

(b) Material which directly or indirectly impugns character, integrity or personal reputation, or directly or indirectly makes charges concerning improper, illegal or immoral conduct or associations, without factual foundation.

(c) Failure to so identify a proxy statement, form of proxy and other soliciting material as to clearly distinguish it from the soliciting material of any other person or persons soliciting for the same meeting or subject matter.

(d) Claims made prior to a meeting regarding the results of a solicitation.

SCHEDULE 14A INFORMATION REQUIRED IN PROXY STATEMENT

Item 7. Remuneration of Directors and Executive Officers

Furnish the information required by Item 402 and Instruction 4 to Item 103 of Regulation S–K if action is to be taken with regard to (i) the election of directors, (ii) any bonus, profit sharing or other remuneration plan, contract, or arrangement in which any director, nominee for election as a director, or officer of the issuer will participate, (iii) any pension or retirement plan in which any such person will participate or (iv) the granting or extension to any such person of any options, warrants or rights to purchase any securities, other than warrants or rights issued to security holders as such, on a pro rata basis. However, if the solicitation is made on behalf of persons other than the issuer, the information required need be furnished only as to nominees of the persons making the solicitation and associates of such nominees.

Item 11. Options, Warrants or Rights

If action is to be taken with respect to the granting or extension of any options, warrants or rights to purchase securities of the issuer or any subsidiary, furnish the following information:

(a) State (i) the title and amount of securities called for or to be called for by such options, warrants or rights; (ii) the prices, expiration dates and other material conditions upon which the options, warrants or rights may be exercised; (iii) the consideration received or to be received by the issuer or subsidiary for the granting of extension of the options, warrants or rights; (iv) the market value of the securities called for or to be called for by the options, warrants or rights as of the latest practicable date, and (v) in the case of options, the Federal income tax consequences of the issuance and exercise of such options to the recipient and to the issuer.

(b) State separately the amount of options, warrants, or rights received or to be received by the following persons, naming each such person: (i) each director or officer named in answer to Item 402(a) of Regulation S–K; (ii) each nominee for election as a director of the issuer; (iii) each associate of such directors, officers or nominees; and (iv) each other person who received or is to receive 5 percent of such options, warrants or rights. State also the total amount of such options, warrants or rights received or to be received by all directors and officers of the issuer as a group, without naming them.

(c) Furnish such information, in addition to that required by this item and Item 402 of Regulation S–K, as may be necessary to describe adequately the provisions already made pursuant to all bonus, profit sharing pension, retirement, stock option, stock purchase, deferred compensation, or other remuneration or incentive plans, now in effect or in effect within the past five years, for (i) each director or officer named in answer to Item 402(a) of Regulation S–K who may participate in the plan to be acted upon; (ii) all present directors and officers of the issuer as a group, if any director or officer may participate in the plan; and (iii) all employees, if employees may participate in the plan.

Item 402 (of Regulation S–K) Management Remuneration and Transactions.

(a) *Remuneration.* Furnish the information required in the table below, in substantially the tabular form specified, concerning all remuneration (except remuneration for which disclosure is required by paragraph (b)(2) or (d) of this Item) paid or distributed through the latest practicable date to, or accrued through such date for the account of, the following persons and group for services in all capacities to the registrant and its subsidiaries during the registrant's last fiscal year, or, in specified instances, certain prior fiscal years.

(1) *Five Executive Officers or Directors.* Each of the five most highly compensated executive officers or directors of the registrant as to whom the total remuneration required to be disclosed in Columns C1 and C2 below would exceed $50,000, naming each such person.

(2) *All Officers and Directors.* All officers and directors of the registrant as a group, stating the number of persons in the group without naming them.

(3) *Specified Tabular Format.*

Remuneration Table

(A)	(B)	(C)		(D)
		Cash and cash-equivalent forms of remuneration		
		(C1)	(C2)	
Name of individual or number of persons in group.	Capacities in which served.	Salaries, fees, directors' fees, commissions, and bonuses.	Securities or property, insurance benefits or reimbursement, personal benefits.	Aggregate of contingent forms of remuneration.

. . .

(c) *Remuneration of Directors.* (1) *Standard Arrangements.* Describe any standard arrangement, stating amounts, by which directors of the registrant are compensated for all services as a director, including any additional amounts payable for committee participation or special assignments.

(2) *Other Arrangements.* If a director of the registrant received remuneration for services as a director during the fiscal year in addition to or in lieu of that specified by any standard arrangement, state the name of the director and the amount of such remuneration earned by each; if this information is given as to an individual named in the table required by paragraph (a), of Item 402, a cross reference may be used.

(d) *Options, Warrants, or Rights.* Furnish the following information specified in paragraphs (d)(1) through (4) immediately following as to all stock appreciation rights and options to purchase securities from the registrant or any of its subsidiaries which were granted to or exercised or realized by each director or executive officer named in answer to paragraph (a)(1) of Item 402, naming each such individual, and all directors and officers of the registrant as a group, without naming them, during the registrant's last fiscal year (or, if applicable, the alternate period specified in either Instruction 5 or Instruction 6 to paragraph (d) of Item 402 and as to all options and stock appreciation rights held by such persons at the end of the last fiscal year (or of such alternate period):

(1) As to options granted during the specified period, state
(i) The title and aggregate amount of securities subject to options;
(ii) The average per share option exercise price; and

(iii) If the option exercise price was less than 100 percent of the market value of the security on the date of grant, such fact and the market price on such date shall be disclosed. The title and aggregate amount of such securities subject to options, if any, which are in tandem with stock appreciation rights should be set forth separately.

(2) As to the exercise or realization of options or stock appreciation rights held in tandem with options granted during the specified period or prior thereto, state the net value of securities (market value less any exercise price) or cash realized during the specified period.

(3) As to all unexercised options or stock appreciation rights in tandem therewith held as of the end of the specified period, state (i) the title and aggregate amount of underlying securities; and (ii) the aggregate potential (unrealized) value of such options or rights, as of the end of the specified period (market value less any exercise or base price). The title and aggregate amount of securities subject to options which are in tandem with stock appreciation rights, if any, shall be set forth separately.

(4) As to stock appreciation rights not in tandem with options, state:

    (i) The number of rights granted during the specified period;

    (ii) The average per share base price thereof;

    (iii) The number of rights outstanding at the end of the specified period;

    (iv) The net value of the shares (market value) or cash realized during the specified period upon exercise or realization of any such rights, granted during the specified period or prior thereto;

    (v) The number of rights outstanding as of the end of the specified period; and

    (vi) The potential (unrealized) value of all such rights outstanding as of the end of the specified period (market value less any base price).

. . .

Item 14. Mergers, Consolidations, Acquisitions and Similar Matters

Furnish the following information if action is to be taken with respect to any plan for (i) the merger or consolidation of the issuer into or with any other person or of any other person into or with the issuer, (ii) the acquisition by the issuer or any of its security holders of securities of another issuer, (iii) the acquisition by the issuer of any other going business or of the assets thereof, (iv) the sale or other transfer of all or any substantial part of the assets of the issuer, or (v) the liquidation or dissolution of the issuer:

(a) Outline briefly the material features of the plan. State the reasons therefor and the general effect thereof upon the rights of existing security holders. If the plan is set forth in a written document, file three copies thereof with the Commission. . . .

(b) Furnish the following information as to the issuer and each person which is to be merged into the issuer or into or with which the issuer is to be merged or consolidated or the business or assets of which are to be acquired or which is the issuer of securities to be acquired by the issuer in exchange for all or a substantial part of its assets or to be acquired by security holders of the issuer. What is required is information essential to an investor's appraisal of the action proposed to be taken.

(1) Describe briefly the business of such person. Information is to be given regarding pertinent matters such as the nature of the products or services, methods of production, markets, methods of distribution and the sources and supply of raw materials.

(2) State the location and describe the general character of the plants and other important physical properties of such person. The description is to be given from an economic and business standpoint, as distinguished from a legal standpoint.

(3) Furnish a brief statement as to dividends in arrears or defaults in principal or interest in respect of any securities of the issuer or of such person, and as to the effect of the plan thereon and such other information as may be appropriate in the particular case to disclose adequately the nature and effect of the proposed action.

(4) Furnish a tabulation in columnar form showing the existing and the pro forma capitalization.

.   .   .

(c) As to each class of securities of the issuer, or of any person specified in paragraph (b) which is admitted to dealing on a national securities exchange or with respect to which a market otherwise exists, and which will be materially affected by the plan, state the high and low sale prices (or, in the absence of trading in a particular period, the range of the bid and asked prices) for each quarterly period within two years. This information may be omitted if the plan involves merely the liquidation or dissolution of the issuer.

.   .   .

D. FEDERAL RULES OF CIVIL PROCEDURE

Rule 23

CLASS ACTIONS

(a) Prerequisites to a Class Action. One or more members of a class may sue or be sued as representative parties on behalf of all only if (1) the class is so numerous that joinder of all members is impracticable, (2) there are questions of law or fact common to the class, (3) the claims or defenses of the representative parties are typical of the claims or defenses of the class, and (4) the representative parties will fairly and adequately protect the interests of the class.

(b) Class Actions Maintainable. An action may be maintained as a class action if the prerequisites of subdivision (a) are satisfied, and in addition:

(1) the prosecution of separate actions by or against individual members of the class would create a risk of

(A) inconsistent or varying adjudications with respect to individual members of the class which would establish incompatible standards of conduct for the party opposing the class, or

(B) adjudications with respect to individual members of the class which would as a practical matter be dispositive of the interests of the other members not parties to the adjudications or substantially impair or impede their ability to protect their interests; or

(2) the party opposing the class has acted or refused to act on grounds generally applicable to the class, thereby making appropriate final injunctive relief or corresponding declaratory relief with respect to the class as a whole; or

(3) the court finds that the questions of law or fact common to the members of the class predominate over any questions affecting only individual members, and that a class action is superior to other available methods for the fair and efficient adjudication of the controversy. The matters pertinent to the findings include: (A) the interest of members of the class in individually controlling the prosecution or defense of separate actions; (B) the extent and nature of any litigation concerning the controversy already commenced by or against members of the class; (C) the desirability or undesirability of concentrating the litigation of the claims in the particular forum; (D) the difficulties likely to be encountered in the management of a class action.

(c) Determination by Order Whether Class Action to be Maintained; Notice; Judgment; Actions Conducted Partially as Class Actions.

(1) As soon as practicable after the commencement of an action brought as a class action, the court shall determine by order whether it is to be so

maintained. An order under this subdivision may be conditional, and may be altered or amended before the decision on the merits.

(2) In any class action maintained under subdivision (b) (3), the court shall direct to the members of the class the best notice practicable under the circumstances, including individual notice to all members who can be identified through reasonable effort. The notice shall advise each member that (A) the court will exclude him from the class if he so requests by a specified date; (B) the judgment, whether favorable or not, will include all members who do not request exclusion; and (C) any member who does not request exclusion may, if he desires, enter an appearance through his counsel.

(3) The judgment in an action maintained as a class action under subdivision (b) (1) or (b) (2), whether or not favorable to the class, shall include and describe those whom the court finds to be members of the class. The judgment in an action maintained as a class action under subdivision (b) (3), whether or not favorable to the class, shall include and specify or describe those to whom the notice provided in subdivision (c) (2) was directed, and who have not requested exclusion, and whom the court finds to be members of the class.

(4) When appropriate (A) an action may be brought or maintained as a class action with respect to particular issues, or (B) a class may be divided into subclasses and each subclass treated as a class, and the provisions of this rule shall then be construed and applied accordingly.

(d) Orders in Conduct of Actions. In the conduct of actions to which this rule applies, the court may make appropriate orders: (1) determining the course of proceedings or prescribing measures to prevent undue repetition or complication in the presentation of evidence or argument; (2) requiring, for the protection of the members of the class or otherwise for the fair conduct of the action, that notice be given in such manner as the court may direct to some or all of the members of any step in the action, or of the proposed extent of the judgment, or of the opportunity of members to signify whether they consider the representation fair and adequate, to intervene and present claims or defenses, or otherwise to come into the action; (3) imposing conditions on the representative parties or on intervenors; (4) requiring that the pleadings be amended to eliminate therefrom allegations as to representation of absent persons, and that the action proceed accordingly; (5) dealing with similar procedural matters. The orders may be combined with an order under Rule 16, and may be altered or amended as may be desirable from time to time.

(e) Dismissal or Compromise. A class action shall not be dismissed or compromised without the approval of the court, and notice of the proposed dismissal or compromise shall be given to all members of the class in such manner as the court directs.

Rule 23.1

DERIVATIVE ACTIONS BY SHAREHOLDERS

In a derivative action brought by one or more shareholders or members to enforce a right of a corporation or of an unincorporated association, the corporation or association having failed to enforce a right which may properly be asserted by it, the complaint shall be verified and shall allege (1) that the plaintiff was a shareholder or member at the time of the transaction of which he complains or that his share or membership thereafter devolved on him by operation of law, and (2) that the action is not a collusive one to confer jurisdiction on a court of the United States which it would not otherwise have. The complaint shall also allege with particularity the efforts, if any, made by the plaintiff to obtain the action he desires from the directors or comparable authority and, if necessary, from the shareholders or members, and the reasons for his failure to obtain the action or for not making the effort. The derivative action may not be maintained if it appears that the plaintiff does not fairly and adequately represent the interests of the shareholders or members similarly situated in enforcing the right of the corporation or association. The action shall not be dismissed or compromised without the approval of the court, and notice of the proposed dismissal or compromise shall be given to shareholders or members in such manner as the court directs.

Rule 23.2

ACTIONS RELATING TO UNINCORPORATED ASSOCIATIONS

An action brought by or against the members of an unincorporated association as a class by naming certain members as representative parties may be maintained only if it appears that the representative parties will fairly and adequately protect the interests of the association and its members. In the conduct of the action the court may make appropriate orders corresponding with those described in Rule 23(d), and the procedure for dismissal or compromise of the action shall correspond with that provided in Rule 23(e).

Part III

STATE STATUTES AND REGULATIONS

A–1. UNIFORM PARTNERSHIP ACT (EXCERPTS)

§ 2. Definition of Terms

In this act, "Court" includes every court and judge having jurisdiction in the case.

"Business" includes every trade, occupation, or profession.

"Person" includes individuals, partnerships, corporations, and other associations.

"Bankrupt" includes bankrupt under the Federal Bankruptcy Act or insolvent under any state insolvent act.

"Conveyance" includes every assignment, lease, mortgage, or encumbrance.

"Real property" includes land and any interest or estate in land.

§ 6. Partnership Defined

(1) A partnership is an association of two or more persons to carry on as co-owners a business for profit.

(2) But any association formed under any other statute of this state, or any statute adopted by authority, other than the authority of this state, is not a partnership under this act, unless such association would have been a partnership in this state prior to the adoption of this act; but this act shall apply to limited partnerships except in so far as the statutes relating to such partnerships are inconsistent herewith.

§ 7. Rules for Determining the Existence of a Partnership

In determining whether a partnership exists, these rules shall apply:

(1) Except as provided by Section 16 persons who are not partners as to each other are not partners as to third persons.

(2) Joint tenancy, tenancy in common, tenancy by the entireties, joint property, common property, or part ownership does not of itself establish a partnership, whether such co-owners do or do not share any profits made by the use of the property.

(3) The sharing of gross returns does not of itself establish a partnership, whether or not the persons sharing them have a joint or common right or interest in any property from which the returns are derived.

(4) The receipt by a person of a share of the profits of a business is prima facie evidence that he is a partner in the business, but no such inference shall be drawn if such profits were received in payment:

(a) As a debt by installments or otherwise,

(b) As wages of an employee or rent to a landlord,

79

(c) As an annuity to a widow or representative of a deceased partner,

(d) As interest on a loan, though the amount of payment vary with the profits of the business,

(e) As the consideration for the sale of a good-will of a business or other property by installments or otherwise.

§ 8. Partnership Property

(1) All property originally brought into the partnership stock or subsequently acquired by purchase or otherwise, on account of the partnership, is partnership property.

(2) Unless the contrary intention appears, property acquired with partnership funds is partnership property.

(3) Any estate in real property may be acquired in the partnership name. Title so acquired can be conveyed only in the partnership name.

(4) A conveyance to a partnership in the partnership name, though without words of inheritance, passes the entire estate of the grantor unless a contrary intent appears.

§ 9. Partner Agent of Partnership as to Partnership Business

(1) Every partner is an agent of the partnership for the purpose of its business, and the act of every partner, including the execution in the partnership name of any instrument, for apparently carrying on in the usual way the business of the partnership of which he is a member binds the partnership, unless the partner so acting has in fact no authority to act for the partnership in the particular matter, and the person with whom he is dealing has knowledge of the fact that he has no such authority.

(2) An act of a partner which is not apparently for the carrying on of the business of the partnership in the usual way does not bind the partnership unless authorized by the other partners.

(3) Unless authorized by the other partners or unless they have abandoned the business, one or more but less than all the partners have no authority to:

(a) Assign the partnership property in trust for creditors or on the assignee's promise to pay the debts of the partnership,

(b) Dispose of the good-will of the business,

(c) Do any other act which would make it impossible to carry on the ordinary business of a partnership,

(d) Confess a judgment,

(e) Submit a partnership claim or liability to arbitration or reference.

(4) No act of a partner in contravention of a restriction on authority shall bind the partnership to persons having knowledge of the restriction.

§ 10. Conveyance of Real Property of the Partnership

(1) Where title to real property is in the partnership name, any partner may convey title to such property by a conveyance executed in the

partnership name; but the partnership may recover such property unless the partner's act binds the partnership under the provisions of paragraph (1) of section 9 or unless such property has been conveyed by the grantee or a person claiming through such grantee to a holder for value without knowledge that the partner, in making the conveyance, has exceeded his authority.

(2) Where title to real property is in the name of the partnership, a conveyance executed by a partner, in his own name, passes the equitable interest of the partnership, provided the act is one within the authority of the partner under the provisions of paragraph (1) of section 9.

(3) Where title to real property is in the name of one or more but not all the partners, and the record does not disclose the right of the partnership, the partners in whose name the title stands may convey title to such property, but the partnership may recover such property if the partners' act does not bind the partnership under the provisions of paragraph (1) of section 9, unless the purchaser, or his assignee, is a holder for value, without knowledge.

(4) Where the title to real property is in the name of one or more or all the partners, or in a third person in trust for the partnership, a conveyance executed by a partner in the partnership name, or in his own name, passes the equitable interest of the partnership, provided the act is one within the authority of the partner under the provisions of paragraph (1) of section 9.

(5) Where the title to real property is in the names of all the partners a conveyance executed by all the partners passes all their rights in such property.

§ 11. Partnership Bound by Admission of Partner

An admission or representation made by any partner concerning partnership affairs within the scope of his authority as conferred by this act is evidence against the partnership.

§ 13. Partnership Bound by Partner's Wrongful Act

Where, by any wrongful act or omission of any partner acting in the ordinary course of the business of the partnership or with the authority of his co-partners, loss or injury is caused to any person, not being a partner in the partnership, or any penalty is incurred, the partnership is liable therefor to the same extent as the partner so acting or omitting to act.

§ 14. Partnership Bound by Partner's Breach of Trust

The partnership is bound to make good the loss:

(a) Where one partner acting within the scope of his apparent authority receives money or property of a third person and misapplies it; and

(b) Where the partnership in the course of its business receives money or property of a third person and the money or property so received is misapplied by any partner while it is in the custody of the partnership.

§ 15. Nature of Partner's Liability

All partners are liable

(a) Jointly and severally for everything chargeable to the partnership under sections 13 and 14.

(b) Jointly for all other debts and obligations of the partnership; but any partner may enter into a separate obligation to perform a partnership contract.

§ 16. Partner by Estoppel

(1) When a person, by words spoken or written or by conduct, represents himself, or consents to another representing him to any one, as a partner in an existing partnership or with one or more persons not actual partners, he is liable to any such person to whom such representation has been made, who has, on the faith of such representation, given credit to the actual or apparent partnership, and if he has made such representation or consented to its being made in a public manner he is liable to such person, whether the representation has or has not been made or communicated to such person so giving credit by or with the knowledge of the apparent partner making the representation or consenting to its being made.

(a) When a partnership liability results, he is liable as though he were an actual member of the partnership.

(b) When no partnership liability results, he is liable jointly with the other persons, if any, so consenting to the contract or representation as to incur liability, otherwise separately.

(2) When a person has been thus represented to be a partner in an existing partnership, or with one or more persons not actual partners, he is an agent of the persons consenting to such representation to bind them to the same extent and in the same manner as though he were a partner in fact, with respect to persons who rely upon the representation. Where all the members of the existing partnership consent to the representation, a partnership act or obligation results; but in all other cases it is the joint act or obligation of the person acting and the persons consenting to the representation.

§ 17. Liability of Incoming Partner

A person admitted as a partner into an existing partnership is liable for all the obligations of the partnership arising before his admission as though he had been a partner when such obligations were incurred, except that this liability shall be satisfied only out of partnership property.

§ 18. Rules Determining Rights and Duties of Partners

The rights and duties of the partners in relation to the partnership shall be determined, subject to any agreement between them, by the following rules:

(a) Each partner shall be repaid his contributions, whether by way of capital or advances to the partnership property and share equally in the profits and surplus remaining after all liabilities, including those to partners, are satisfied; and must contribute towards the losses, whether of capital or otherwise, sustained by the partnership according to his share in the profits.

(b) The partnership must indemnify every partner in respect of payments made and personal liabilities reasonably incurred by him in the ordinary and proper conduct of its business, or for the preservation of its business or property.

(c) A partner, who in aid of the partnership makes any payment or advance beyond the amount of capital which he agreed to contribute, shall be paid interest from the date of the payment or advance.

(d) A partner shall receive interest on the capital contributed by him only from the date when repayment should be made.

(e) All partners have equal rights in the management and conduct of the partnership business.

(f) No partner is entitled to remuneration for acting in the partnership business, except that a surviving partner is entitled to reasonable compensation for his services in winding up the partnership affairs.

(g) No person can become a member of a partnership without the consent of all the partners.

(h) Any difference arising as to ordinary matters connected with the partnership business may be decided by a majority of the partners; but no act in contravention of any agreement between the partners may be done rightfully without the consent of all the partners.

§ 21. Partner Accountable as a Fiduciary

(1) Every partner must account to the partnership for any benefit, and hold as trustee for it any profits derived by him without the consent of the other partners from any transaction connected with the formation, conduct, or liquidation of the partnership or from any use by him of its property.

(2) This section applies also to the representatives of a deceased partner engaged in the liquidation of the affairs of the partnership as the personal representatives of the last surviving partner.

§ 25. Nature of a Partner's Right in Specific Partnership Property

(1) A partner is co-owner with his partners of specific partnership property holding as a tenant in partnership.

(2) The incidents of this tenancy are such that:

(a) A partner, subject to the provisions of this act and to any agreement between the partners, has an equal right with his partners to possess specific partnership property for partnership purposes; but he has no right to possess such property for any other purpose without the consent of his partners.

(b) A partner's right in specific partnership property is not assignable except in connection with the assignment of rights of all the partners in the same property.

(c) A partner's right in specific partnership property is not subject to attachment or execution, except on a claim against the partnership. When partnership property is attached for a partnership debt the partners, or any of them, or the representatives of a deceased partner, cannot claim any right under the homestead or exemption laws.

(d) On the death of a partner his right in specific partnership property vests in the surviving partner or partners, except where the deceased was the last surviving partner, when his right in such property vests in his legal representative. Such surviving partner or partners, or the legal representative of the last surviving partner, has no right to possess the partnership property for any but a partnership purpose.

(e) A partner's right in specific partnership property is not subject to dower, curtesy, or allowances to widows, heirs, or next of kin.

§ 26. Nature of Partner's Interest in the Partnership

A partner's interest in the partnership is his share of the profits and surplus, and the same is personal property.

§ 27. Assignment of Partner's Interest

(1) A conveyance by a partner of his interest in the partnership does not of itself dissolve the partnership, nor, as against the other partners in the absence of agreement, entitle the assignee, during the continuance of the partnership, to interfere in the management or administration of the partnership business or affairs, or to require any information or account of partnership transactions, or to inspect the partnership books; but it merely entitles the assignee to receive in accordance with his contract the profits to which the assigning partner would otherwise be entitled.

(2) In case of a dissolution of the partnership, the assignee is entitled to receive his assignor's interest and may require an account from the date only of the last account agreed to by all the partners.

§ 28. Partner's Interest Subject to Charging Order

(1) On due application to a competent court by any judgment creditor of a partner, the court which entered the judgment, order, or decree, or any other court, may charge the interest of the debtor partner with payment of the unsatisfied amount of such judgment debt with interest thereon; and may then or later appoint a receiver of his share of the profits, and of any other money due or to fall due to him in respect of the partnership, and make all other orders, directions, accounts and inquiries which the debtor partner might have made, or which the circumstances of the case may require.

(2) The interest charged may be redeemed at any time before foreclosure, or in case of a sale being directed by the court may be purchased without thereby causing a dissolution:

(a) With separate property, by any one or more of the partners, or

(b) With partnership property, by any one or more of the partners with the consent of all the partners whose interests are not so charged or sold.

(3) Nothing in this act shall be held to deprive a partner of his right, if any, under the exemption laws, as regards his interest in the partnership.

§ 29. Dissolution Defined

The dissolution of a partnership is the change in the relation of the partners caused by any partner ceasing to be associated in the carrying on as distinguished from the winding up of the business.

§ 31. Causes of Dissolution

Dissolution is caused: (1) Without violation of the agreement between the partners,

(a) By the termination of the definite term or particular undertaking specified in the agreement,

(b) By the express will of any partner when no definite term or particular undertaking is specified,

(c) By the express will of all the partners who have not assigned their interests or suffered them to be charged for their separate debts, either before or after the termination of any specified term or particular undertaking,

(d) By the expulsion of any partner from the business bona fide in accordance with such a power conferred by the agreement between the partners;

(2) In contravention of the agreement between the partners, where the circumstances do not permit a dissolution under any other provision of this section, by the express will of any partner at any time;

(3) By any event which makes it unlawful for the business of the partnership to be carried on or for the members to carry it on in partnership;

(4) By the death of any partner;

(5) By the bankruptcy of any partner or the partnership;

(6) By decree of court under section 32.

§ 32. Dissolution by Decree of Court

(1) On application by or for a partner the court shall decree a dissolution whenever:

(a) A partner has been declared a lunatic in any judicial proceeding or is shown to be of unsound mind,

(b) A partner becomes in any other way incapable of performing his part of the partnership contract,

(c) A partner has been guilty of such conduct as tends to affect prejudicially the carrying on of the business,

(d) A partner wilfully or persistently commits a breach of the partnership agreement, or otherwise so conducts himself in matters relating to the partnership business that it is not reasonably practicable to carry on the business in partnership with him,

(e) The business of the partnership can only be carried on at a loss,

(f) Other circumstances render a dissolution equitable.

(2) On the application of the purchaser of a partner's interest under sections 28 or 29.[13]

(a) After the termination of the specified term or particular undertaking,

(b) At any time if the partnership was a partnership at will when the interest was assigned or when the charging order was issued.

§ 33.   General Effect of Dissolution on Authority of Partner

Except so far as may be necessary to wind up partnership affairs or to complete transactions begun but not then finished, dissolution terminates all authority of any partner to act for the partnership,

(1) With respect to the partners,

(a) When the dissolution is not by the act, bankruptcy or death of a partner; or

(b) When the dissolution is by such act, bankruptcy or death of a partner, in cases were section 34 so requires.

(2) With respect to persons not partners, as declared in section 35.

§ 34.   Right of Partner to Contribution From Copartners After Dissolution

Where the dissolution is caused by the act, death or bankruptcy of a partner, each partner is liable to his copartners for his share of any liability created by any partner acting for the partnership as if the partnership had not been dissolved unless

(a) The dissolution being by act of any partner, the partner acting for the partnership had knowledge of the dissolution, or

(b) The dissolution being by the death or bankruptcy of a partner, the partner acting for the partnership had knowledge or notice of the death or bankruptcy.

§ 35.   Power of Partner to Bind Partnership to Third Persons After Dissolution

(1) After dissolution a partner can bind the partnership except as provided in Paragraph (3)

(a) By any act appropriate for winding up partnership affairs or completing transactions unfinished at dissolution;

(b) By any transaction which would bind the partnership if dissolution had not taken place, provided the other party to the transaction

(I) Had extended credit to the partnership prior to dissolution and had no knowledge or notice of the dissolution; or

13. A footnote in the annotated edition states: "So in the original. Probably should read 'Sections 27 or 28.'"

(II) Though he had not so extended credit, had nevertheless known of the partnership prior to dissolution, and, having no knowledge or notice of dissolution, the fact of dissolution had not been advertised in a newspaper of general circulation in the place (or in each place if more than one) at which the partnership business was regularly carried on.

(2) The liability of a partner under paragraph (1b) shall be satisfied out of partnership assets alone when such partner had been prior to dissolution

(a) Unknown as a partner to the person with whom the contract is made; and

(b) So far unknown and inactive in partnership affairs that the business reputation of the partnership could not be said to have been in any degree due to his connection with it.

(3) The partnership is in no case bound by any act of a partner after dissolution

(a) Where the partnership is dissolved because it is unlawful to carry on the business, unless the act is appropriate for winding up partnership affairs; or

(b) Where the partner has become bankrupt; or

(c) Where the partner has no authority to wind up partnership affairs; except by a transaction with one who

(I) Had extended credit to the partnership prior to dissolution and had no knowledge or notice of his want of authority; or

(II) Had not extended credit to the partnership prior to dissolution, and, having no knowledge or notice of his want of authority, the fact of his want of authority has not been advertised in the manner provided for advertising the fact of dissolution in paragraph (1bII).

(4) Nothing in this section shall affect the liability under section 16 of any person who after dissolution represents himself or consents to another representing him as a partner in a partnership engaged in carrying on business.

§ 36. Effect of Dissolution on Partner's Existing Liability

(1) The dissolution of the partnership does not of itself discharge the existing liability of any partner.

(2) A partner is discharged from any existing liability upon dissolution of the partnership by an agreement to that effect between himself, the partnership creditor and the person or partnership continuing the business; and such agreement may be inferred from the course of dealing between the creditor having knowledge of the dissolution and the person or partnership continuing the business.

(3) Where a person agrees to assume the existing obligations of a dissolved partnership, the partners whose obligations have been assumed shall be discharged from any liability to any creditor of the partnership who,

knowing of the agreement, consents to a material alteration in the nature or time of payment of such obligations.

(4) The individual property of a deceased partner shall be liable for all obligations of the partnership incurred while he was a partner but subject to the prior payment of his separate debts.

§ 37. Right to Wind Up

Unless otherwise agreed the partners who have not wrongfully dissolved the partnership or the legal representative of the last surviving partner, not bankrupt, has the right to wind up the partnership affairs; provided, however, that any partner, his legal representative or his assignee, upon cause shown, may obtain winding up by the court.

§ 38. Rights of Partners to Application of Partnership Property

(1) When dissolution is caused in any way, except in contravention of the partnership agreement, each partner as against his co-partners and all persons claiming through them in respect of their interests in the partnership, unless otherwise agreed, may have the partnership property applied to discharge its liabilities, and the surplus applied to pay in cash the net amount owing to the respective partners.   But if dissolution is caused by expulsion of a partner, bona fide under the partnership agreement and if the expelled partner is discharged from all partnership liabilities, either by payment or agreement under section 36(2), he shall receive in cash only the net amount due him from the partnership.

(2) When dissolution is caused in contravention of the partnership agreement the rights of the partners shall be as follows:

(a) Each partner who has not caused dissolution wrongfully shall have,

(I) All the rights specified in paragraph (1) of this section, and

(II) The right, as against each partner who has caused the dissolution wrongfully, to damages for breach of the agreement.

(b) The partners who have not caused the dissolution wrongfully, if they all desire to continue the business in the same name, either by themselves or jointly with others, may do so, during the agreed term for the partnership and for that purpose may possess the partnership property, provided they secure the payment by bond approved by the court, or pay to any partner who has caused the dissolution wrongfully, the value of his interest in the partnership at the dissolution, less any damages recoverable under clause (2aII) of this section, and in like manner indemnify him against all present or future partnership liabilities.

(c) A partner who has caused the dissolution wrongfully shall have:

(I) If the business is not continued under the provisions of paragraph (2b) all the rights of a partner under paragraph (1), subject to clause (2aII), of this section,

(II) If the business is continued under paragraph (2b) of this section the right as against his co-partners and all claiming through them in respect of their interests in the partnership, to have the value of his interest in the partnership, less any damages caused to his co-partners by the dissolution, ascertained and paid to him in cash, or the payment secured by bond approved by the court, and to be released from all existing liabilities of the partnership; but in ascertaining the value of the partner's interest the value of the good-will of the business shall not be considered.

§ 40. Rules for Distribution

In settling accounts between the partners after dissolution, the following rules shall be observed, subject to any agreement to the contrary:

(a) The assets of the partnership are:

(I) The partnership property,

(II) The contributions of the partners necessary for the payment of all the liabilities specified in clause (b) of this paragraph.

(b) The liabilities of the partnership shall rank in order of payment, as follows:

(I) Those owing to creditors other than partners,

(II) Those owing to partners other than for capital and profits,

(III) Those owing to partners in respect of capital,

(IV) Those owing to partners in respect of profits.

(c) The assets shall be applied in the order of their declaration in clause (a) of this paragraph to the satisfaction of the liabilities.

(d) The partners shall contribute, as provided by section 18(a) the amount necessary to satisfy the liabilities; but if any, but not all, of the partners are insolvent, or, not being subject to process, refuse to contribute, the other parties shall contribute their share of the liabilities, and, in the relative proportions in which they share the profits, the additional amount necessary to pay the liabilities.

(e) An assignee for the benefit of creditors or any person appointed by the court shall have the right to enforce the contributions specified in clause (d) of this paragraph.

(f) Any partner or his legal representative shall have the right to enforce the contributions specified in clause (d) of this paragraph, to the extent of the amount which he has paid in excess of his share of the liability.

(g) The individual property of a deceased partner shall be liable for the contributions specified in clause (d) of this paragraph.

(h) When partnership property and the individual properties of the partners are in possession of a court for distribution, partnership creditors shall have priority on partnership property and separate creditors on individual property, saving the rights of lien or secured creditors as heretofore.

(i) Where a partner has become bankrupt or his estate is insolvent the claims against his separate property shall rank in the following order:

(I) Those owing to separate creditors,

(II) Those owing to partnership creditors,

(III) Those owing to partners by way of contribution.

§ 41. Liability of Persons Continuing the Business in Certain Cases

(1) When any new partner is admitted into an existing partnership, or when any partner retires and assigns (or the representative of the deceased partner assigns) his rights in partnership property to two or more of the partners, or to one or more of the partners and one or more third persons, if the business is continued without liquidation of the partnership affairs, creditors of the first or dissolved partnership are also creditors of the partnership so continuing the business.

A–2. UNIFORM LIMITED PARTNERSHIP ACT (EXCERPTS)[14]

§ 1. Limited Partnership Defined

A limited partnership is a partnership formed by two or more persons under the provisions of Section 2, having as members one or more general partners and one or more limited partners. The limited partners as such shall not be bound by the obligations of the partnership.

§ 2. Formation

(1) Two or more persons desiring to form a limited partnership shall

(a) Sign and swear to a certificate, which shall state

    I. The name of the partnership,

    II. The character of the business,

    III. The location of the principal place of business,

    IV. The name and place of residence of each member; general and limited partners being respectively designated,

    V. The term for which the partnership is to exist,

    VI. The amount of cash and a description of and the agreed value of the other property contributed by each limited partner,

    VII. The additional contributions, if any, agreed to be made by each limited partner and the times at which or events on the happening of which they shall be made,

    VIII. The time, if agreed upon, when the contribution of each limited partner is to be returned,

    IX. The share of the profits or the other compensation by way of income which each limited partner shall receive by reason of his contribution,

    X. The right, if given, of a limited partner to substitute an assignee as contributor in his place, and the terms and conditions of the substitution.

14. The National Conference of Commissioners on Uniform State Laws in 1976 approved a Revised Uniform Limited Partnership Act. As of January 1982 it had been adopted by seven states. The treatment in its § 303 of the problems addressed by § 7 of the 1916 version is so much more detailed that it is included in brackets immediately following that section.

XI. The right, if given, of the partners to admit additional limited partners,

XII. The right, if given, of one or more of the limited partners to priority over other limited partners, as to contributions or as to compensation by way of income, and the nature of such priority,

XIII. The right, if given, of the remaining general partner or partners to continue the business on the death, retirement or insanity of a general partner, and

XIV. The right, if given, of a limited partner to demand and receive property other than cash in return for his contribution.

(b) File for record the certificate in the office of [here designate the proper office].

(2) A limited partnership is formed if there has been substantial compliance in good faith with the requirements of paragraph (1).

§ 7. Limited Partner not Liable to Creditors

A limited partner shall not become liable as a general partner unless, in addition to the exercise of his rights and powers as a limited partner, he takes part in the control of the business.

[§ 303 of 1976 Version. Liability to Third Parties

(a) Except as provided in subsection (d), a limited partner is not liable for the obligations of a limited partnership unless he is also a general partner or, in addition to the exercise of his rights and powers as a limited partner, he takes part in the control of the business. However, if the limited partner's participation in the control of the business is not substantially the same as the exercise of the powers of a general partner, he is liable only to persons who transact business with the limited partnership with actual knowledge of his participation in control.

(b) A limited partner does not participate in the control of the business within the meaning of subsection (a) solely by doing one or more of the following:

(1) being a contractor for or an agent or employee of the limited partnership or of a general partner;

(2) consulting with and advising a general partner with respect to the business of the limited partnership;

(3) acting as surety for the limited partnership;

(4) approving or disapproving an amendment to the partnership agreement; or

(5) voting on one or more of the following matters:

(i) the dissolution and winding up of the limited partnership;

(ii) the sale, exchange, lease, mortgage, pledge, or other transfer of all or substantially all of the assets of the limited partnership other than in the ordinary course of its business;

(iii) the incurrence of indebtedness by the limited partnership other than in the ordinary course of its business;

(iv) a change in the nature of the business; or

(v) the removal of a general partner.

(c) The enumeration in subsection (b) does not mean that the possession or exercise of any other powers by a limited partner constitutes participation by him in the business of the limited partnership.

(d) A limited partner who knowingly permits his name to be used in the name of the limited partnership, except under circumstances permitted by Section 102(2)(i), is liable to creditors who extend credit to the limited partnership without actual knowledge that the limited partner is not a general partner.]

§ 10. Rights of a Limited Partner

(1) A limited partner shall have the same rights as a general partner to

(a) Have the partnership books kept at the principal place of business of the partnership, and at all times to inspect and copy any of them.

(b) Have on demand true and full information of all things affecting the partnership, and a formal account of partnership affairs whenever circumstances render it just and reasonable, and

(c) Have dissolution and winding up by decree of court.

(2) A limited partner shall have the right to receive a share of the profits or other compensation by way of income, and to the return of his contribution as provided in Sections 15 and 16.

§ 11. Status of Person Erroneously Believing Himself a Limited Partner

A person who has contributed to the capital of a business conducted by a person or partnership erroneously believing that he has become a limited partner in a limited partnership, is not, by reason of his exercise of the rights of a limited partner, a general partner with the person or in the partnership carrying on the business, or bound by the obligations of such person or partnership; provided that on ascertaining the mistake he promptly renounces his interest in the profits of the business, or other compensation by way of income.

§ 23. Distribution of Assets

(1) In setting accounts after dissolution the liabilities of the partnership shall be entitled to payment in the following order:

(a) Those to creditors, in the order of priority as provided by law, except those to limited partners on account of their contributions, and to general partners,

(b) Those to limited partners in respect to their share of the profits and other compensation by way of income on their contributions,

(c) Those to limited partners in respect to the capital of their contributions,

(d) Those to general partners other than for capital and profits,

(e) Those to general partners in respect to profits,

(f) Those to general partners in respect to capital.

(2) Subject to any statement in the certificate or to subsequent agreement, limited partners share in the partnership assets in respect to their claims for capital, and in respect to their claims for profits or for compen-

sation by way of income on their contributions respectively, in proportion to the respective amounts of such claims.

§ 24. When Certificate Shall be Cancelled or Amended

(1) The certificate shall be cancelled when the partnership is dissolved or all limited partners cease to be such.

(2) A certificate shall be amended when

(a) There is a change in the name of the partnership or in the amount or character of the contribution of any limited partner,

(b) A person is substituted as a limited partner,

(c) An additional limited partner is admitted,

(d) A person is admitted as a general partner,

(e) A general partner retires, dies or becomes insane, and the business is continued under Section 20,

(f) There is a change in the character of the business of the partnership,

(g) There is a false or erroneous statement in the certificate,

(h) There is a change in the time as stated in the certificate for the dissolution of the partnership or for the return of a contribution,

(i) A time is fixed for the dissolution of the partnership, or the return of a contribution, no time having been specified in the certificate, or

(j) The members desire to make a change in any other statement in the certificate in order that it shall accurately represent the agreement between them.

B.   RESTATEMENT, SECOND, AGENCY (EXCERPTS)

§ 1.   Agency; Principal; Agent

(1) Agency is the fiduciary relation which results from the manifestation of consent by one person to another that the other shall act on his behalf and subject to his control, and consent by the other so to act.

(2) The one for whom action is to be taken is the principal.

(3) The one who is to act is the agent.

§ 2.   Master; Servant; Independent Contractor

(1) A master is a principal who employs an agent to perform service in his affairs and who controls or has the right to control the physical conduct of the other in the performance of the service.

(2) A servant is an agent employed by a master to perform service in his affairs whose physical conduct in the performance of the service is controlled or is subject to the right to control by the master.

(3) An independent contractor is a person who contracts with another to do something for him but who is not controlled by the other nor sub-

ject to the other's right to control with respect to his physical conduct in the performance of the undertaking. He may or may not be an agent.

§ 3. General Agent; Special Agent

(1) A general agent is an agent authorized to conduct a series of transactions involving a continuity of service.

(2) A special agent is an agent authorized to conduct a single transaction or a series of transactions not involving continuity of service.

§ 5. Subagents and Subservants

(1) A subagent is a person appointed by an agent empowered to do so, to perform functions undertaken by the agent for the principal, but for whose conduct the agent agrees with the principal to be primarily responsible.

(2) A subservant is a person appointed by a servant empowered to do so, to perform functions undertaken by the servant for the master and subject to the control as to his physical conduct both by the master and by the servant, but for whose conduct the servant agrees with the principal to be primarily responsible.

§ 7. Authority

Authority is the power of the agent to affect the legal relations of the principal by acts done in accordance with the principal's manifestations of consent to him.

§ 8. Apparent Authority

Apparent authority is the power to affect the legal relations of another person by transactions with third persons, professedly as agent for the other, arising from and in accordance with the other's manifestations to such third persons.

§ 8A. Inherent Agency Power

Inherent agency power is a term used in the restatement of this subject to indicate the power of an agent which is derived not from authority, apparent authority or estoppel, but solely from the agency relation and exists for the protection of persons harmed by or dealing with a servant or other agent.

§ 13. Agent as a Fiduciary

An agent is a fiduciary with respect to matters within the scope of his agency.

§ 14. Control by Principal

A principal has the right to control the conduct of the agent with respect to matters entrusted to him.

§ 14H. Agents or Holders of a Power Given for Their Benefit

One who holds a power created in the form of an agency authority, but given for the benefit of the power holder or of a third person, is not an agent of the one creating the power.

§ 26. Creation of Authority; General Rule

Except for the execution of instruments under seal or for the performance of transactions required by statute to be authorized in a particular way, authority to do an act can be created by written or spoken words or other conduct of the principal which, reasonably interpreted, causes the agent to believe that the principal desires him so to act on the principal's account.

§ 27. Creation of Apparent Authority: General Rule

Except for the execution of instruments under seal or for the conduct of transactions required by statute to be authorized in a particular way, apparent authority to do an act is created as to a third person by written or spoken words or any other conduct of the principal which, reasonably interpreted, causes the third person to believe that the principal consents to have the act done on his behalf by the person purporting to act for him.

§ 82. Ratification

Ratification is the affirmance by a person of a prior act which did not bind him but which was done or professedly done on his account, whereby the act, as to some or all persons, is given effect as if originally authorized by him.

§ 83. Affirmance `

Affirmance is either

(a) a manifestation of an election by one on whose account an unauthorized act has been done to treat the act as authorized, or

(b) conduct by him justifiable only if there were such an election.

§ 118. Revocation or Renunciation

Authority terminates if the principal or the agent manifests to the other dissent to its continuance.

§ 139. Termination of Powers Given as Security

(1) Unless otherwise agreed, a power given as security is not terminated by:

(a) revocation by the creator of the power;

(b) surrender by the holder of the power, if he holds for the benefit of another;

(c) the loss of capacity during the lifetime of either the creator of the power or the holder of the power; or

(d) the death of the holder of the power, or, if the power is given as security for a duty which does not terminate at the death of the creator of the power, by his death.

(2) A power given as security is terminated by its surrender by the beneficiary, if of full capacity; or by the happening of events which, by its terms, discharges the obligations secured by it, or which makes its execution illegal or impossible.

§ 144. General Rule

A disclosed or partially disclosed principal is subject to liability upon contracts made by an agent acting within his authority if made in proper form and with the understanding that the principal is a party.

§ 145. Authorized Representations

In actions brought upon a contract or to rescind a contract or conveyance to which he is a party, a disclosed or partially disclosed principal is responsible for authorized representations of an agent made in connection with it as if made by himself, subject to the rules as to the effect of knowledge of, and notifications given to, the agent.

§ 159. Apparent Authority

A disclosed or partially disclosed principal is subject to liability upon contracts made by an agent acting within his apparent authority if made in proper form and with the understanding that the apparent principal is a party. The rules as to the liability of a principal for authorized acts, are applicable to unauthorized acts which are apparently authorized.

§ 160. Violation of Secret Instructions

A disclosed or partially disclosed principal authorizing an agent to make a contract, but imposing upon him limitations as to incidental terms intended not to be revealed, is subject to liability upon a contract made in violation of such limitations with a third person who has no notice of them.

§ 161. Unauthorized Acts of General Agent

A general agent for a disclosed or partially disclosed principal subjects his principal to liability for acts done on his account which usually accompany or are incidental to transactions which the agent is authorized to conduct if, although they are forbidden by the principal, the other party reasonably believes that the agent is authorized to do them and has no notice that he is not so authorized.

§ 161A. Unauthorized Acts of Special Agents

A special agent for a disclosed or partly disclosed principal has no power to bind his principal by contracts or conveyances which he is not authorized or apparently authorized to make, unless the principal is estopped, or unless:

(a) the agent's only departure from his authority or apparent authority is

    i.   in naming or disclosing the principal, or

    ii.   in having an improper motive, or

iii.   in being negligent in determining the facts upon which his authority is based, or

iv.   in making misrepresentations; or

(b) the agent is given possession of goods or commercial documents with authority to deal with them.

§ 329.   Agent Who Warrants Authority

A person who purports to make a contract, conveyance or representation on behalf of another who has full capacity but whom he has no power to bind, thereby becomes subject to liability to the other party thereto upon an implied warranty of authority, unless he has manifested that he does not make such warranty or the other party knows that the agent is not so authorized.

§ 386.   Duties after Termination of Authority

Unless otherwise agreed, an agent is subject to a duty not to act as such after the termination of his authority.

§ 387.   General Principle

Unless otherwise agreed, an agent is subject to a duty to his principal to act solely for the benefit of the principal in all matters connected with his agency.

§ 388.   Duty to Account for Profits Arising out of Employment

Unless otherwise agreed, an agent who makes a profit in connection with transactions conducted by him on behalf of the principal is under a duty to give such profit to the principal.

§ 389.   Acting as Adverse Party without Principal's Consent

Unless otherwise agreed, an agent is subject to a duty not to deal with his principal as an adverse party in a transaction connected with his agency without the principal's knowledge.

§ 390.   Acting as Adverse Party with Principal's Consent

An agent who, to the knowledge of the principal, acts on his own account in a transaction in which he is employed has a duty to deal fairly with the principal and to disclose to him all facts which the agent knows or should know would reasonably affect the principal's judgment, unless the principal has manifested that he knows such facts or that he does not care to know them.

§ 391.   Acting for Adverse Party without Principal's Consent

Unless otherwise agreed, an agent is subject to a duty to his principal not to act on behalf of an adverse party in a transaction connected with his agency without the principal's knowledge.

§ 392. Acting for Adverse Party with Principal's Consent

An agent who, to the knowledge of two principals, acts for both of them in a transaction between them, has a duty to act with fairness to each and to disclose to each all facts which he knows or should know would reasonably affect the judgment of each in permitting such dual agency, except as to a principal who has manifested that he knows such facts or does not care to know them.

§ 393. Competition as to Subject Matter of Agency

Unless otherwise agreed, an agent is subject to a duty not to compete with the principal concerning the subject matter of his agency.

§ 394. Acting for One with Conflicting Interests

Unless otherwise agreed, an agent is subject to a duty not to act or to agree to act during the period of his agency for persons whose interests conflict with those of the principal in matters in which the agent is employed.

§ 395. Using or Disclosing Confidential Information

Unless otherwise agreed, an agent is subject to a duty to the principal not to use or to communicate information confidentially given him by the principal or acquired by him during the course of or on account of his agency or in violation of his duties as agent, in competition with or to the injury of the principal, on his own account or on behalf of another, although such information does not relate to the transaction in which he is then employed, unless the information is a matter of general knowledge.

§ 396. Using Confidential Information after Termination of Agency

Unless otherwise agreed, after the termination of the agency, the agent:

(a) has no duty not to compete with the principal;

(b) has a duty to the principal not to use or to disclose to third persons, on his own account or on account of others, in competition with the principal or to his injury, trade secrets, written lists of names, or other similar confidential matters given to him only for the principal's use or acquired by the agent in violation of duty. The agent is entitled to use general information concerning the method of business of the principal and the names of the customers retained in his memory, if not acquired in violation of his duty as agent;

(c) has a duty to account for profits made by the sale or use of trade secrets and other confidential information, whether or not in competition with the principal;

(d) has a duty to the principal not to take advantage of a still subsisting confidential relation created during the prior agency relation.

§ 438. Duty of Indemnity; the Principle

(1) A principal is under a duty to indemnify the agent in accordance with the terms of the agreement with him.

(2) In the absence of terms to the contrary in the agreement of employment, the principal has a duty to indemnify the agent where the agent

(a) makes a payment authorized or made necessary in executing the principal's affairs or, unless he is officious, one beneficial to the principal, or

(b) suffers a loss which, because of their relation, it is fair that the principal should bear.

§ 439. When Duty of Indemnity Exists

Unless otherwise agreed, a principal is subject to a duty to exonerate an agent who is not barred by the illegality of his conduct to indemnify him for:

(a) authorized payments made by the agent on behalf of the principal;

(b) payments upon contracts upon which the agent is authorized to make himself liable, and upon obligations arising from the possession or ownership of things which he is authorized to hold on account of the principal;

(c) payments of damages to third persons which he is required to make on account of the authorized performance of an act which constitutes a tort or a breach of contract;

(d) expenses of defending actions by third persons brought because of the agent's authorized conduct, such actions being unfounded but not brought in bad faith; and

(e) payments resulting in benefit to the principal, made by the agent under such circumstances that it would be inequitable for indemnity not to be made.

§ 440. When No Duty of Indemnity

Unless otherwise agreed, the principal is not subject to a duty to indemnify an agent:

(a) for pecuniary loss or other harm, not of benefit to the principal, arising from the performance of unauthorized acts or resulting solely from the agent's negligence or other fault; or

(b) if the principal has otherwise performed his duties to the agent, for physical harm caused by the performance of authorized acts, for harm suffered as a result of torts, other than the tortious institution of suits, committed upon the agent by third persons because of his employment, or for harm suffered by the refusal of third persons to deal with him; or

(c) if the agent's loss resulted from an enterprise which he knew to be illegal.

C. SELECTED NEW YORK STATUTES

BUSINESS CORPORATION LAW

§ 626. Shareholders' derivative action brought in the right of the corporation to procure a judgment in its favor

(a) An action may be brought in the right of a domestic or foreign corporation to procure a judgment in its favor, by a holder of shares or of voting trust certificates of the corporation or of a beneficial interest in such shares or certificates.

(b) In any such action, it shall be made to appear that the plaintiff is such a holder at the time of bringing the action and that he was such a holder at the time of the transaction of which he complains, or that his shares or his interest therein devolved upon him by operation of law.

(c) In any such action, the complaint shall set forth with particularity the efforts of the plaintiff to secure the initiation of such action by the board or the reasons for not making such effort.

(d) Such action shall not be discontinued, compromised or settled, without the approval of the court having jurisdiction of the action. If the court shall determine that the interests of the shareholders or any class or classes thereof will be substantially affected by such discontinuance, compromise, or settlement, the court, in its discretion, may direct that notice, by publication or otherwise, shall be given to the shareholders or class or classes thereof whose interests it determines will be so affected; if notice is so directed to be given, the court may determine which one or more of the parties to the action shall bear the expense of giving the same, in such amount as the court shall determine and find to be reasonable in the circumstances, and the amount of such expense shall be awarded as special costs of the action and recoverable in the same manner as statutory taxable costs.

(e) If the action on behalf of the corporation was successful, in whole or in part, or if anything was received by the plaintiff or plaintiffs or a claimant or claimants as the result of a judgment, compromise or settlement of an action or claim, the court may award the plaintiff or plaintiffs, claimant or claimants, reasonable expenses, including reasonable attorney's fees, and shall direct him or them to account to the corporation for the remainder of the proceeds so received by him or them. This paragraph shall not apply to any judgment rendered for the benefit of injured shareholders only and limited to a recovery of the loss or damage sustained by them.

§ 627. Security for expenses in shareholders' derivative action brought in the right of the corporation to procure a judgment in its favor

In any action specified in section 626 (Shareholders' derivative action brought in the right of the corporation to procure a judgment in its favor), if the plaintiff or plaintiffs hold less than five percent of any class of the outstanding shares or hold voting trust certificates or a beneficial interest in shares representing less than five percent of any class of such shares, then unless the shares, voting trust certificates and beneficial interest of such plaintiff or plaintiffs have a fair value in excess of fifty thousand dollars, the corporation in whose right such action is brought shall be entitled at any stage of the proceedings before final judgment to require the plaintiff or plaintiffs to give security for the reasonable expenses, including attorney's fees, which may be incurred by it in connection with such action and by the other parties defendant in connection therewith for which the corporation may become liable under this chapter, under any contract, or otherwise under law, to which the corporation shall have recourse in such amount as the court having jurisdiction of such action shall determine upon the termination of such action. The amount of such security may thereafter from time to time be increased or decreased in the discretion of the court having jurisdiction of such action upon showing that the security provided has or may become inadequate or excessive.

§ 721. Exclusivity of statutory provisions for indemnification of directors and officers

No provision made to indemnify directors or officers for the defense of any civil or criminal action or proceeding, whether contained in the certificate of incorporation, the by-laws, a resolution of shareholders or directors, an agreement or otherwise, nor any award of indemnification by a court, shall be valid unless consistent with this article. Nothing contained in this article shall affect any rights to indemnification to which corporate personnel other than directors and officers may be entitled by contract or otherwise under law.

§ 722. Authorization for indemnification of directors and officers in actions by or in the right of a corporation to procure a judgment in its favor

(a) A corporation may indemnify any person, made a party to an action by or in the right of the corporation to procure a judgment in its favor by reason of the fact that he, his testator or intestate, is or was a director or officer of the corporation, against the reasonable expenses, including attorneys' fees, actually and necessarily incurred by him in connection with the defense of such action, or in connection with an appeal therein, except in relation to matters as to which such director or officer is adjudged to have breached his duty to the corporation under section 717 (Duty of directors) or under paragraph (h) of Section 715 (officers).

(b) The indemnification authorized under paragraph (a) shall in no case include:

(1) Amounts paid in settling or otherwise disposing of a threatened action, or a pending action with or without court approval, or

(2) Expenses incurred in defending a threatened action, or a pending action which is settled or otherwise disposed of without court approval.

§ 723. Authorization for indemnification of directors and officers in actions or proceedings other than by or in the right of a corporation to procure a judgment in its favor

(a) A corporation may indemnify any person, made, or threatened to be made, a party to an action or proceeding other than one by or in the right of the corporation to procure a judgment in its favor, whether civil or criminal, including an action by or in the right of any other corporation of any type or kind, domestic or foreign, or any partnership, joint venture, trust, employee benefit plan or other enterprise, which any director or officer of the corporation served in any capacity at the request of the corporation, by reason of the fact that he, his testator or intestate, was a director or officer of the corporation, or served such other corporation, partnership, joint venture, trust, employee benefit plan or other enterprise in any capacity, against judgments, fines, amounts paid in settlement and reasonable expenses, including attorneys' fees actually and necessarily incurred as a result of such action or proceeding, or any appeal therein, if such director or officer acted, in good faith, for a purpose which he reasonably believed to be in, or, in the case of service for any other corporation or any partnership, joint venture, trust, employee benefit plan or other enterprise, not opposed to, the best interests of the corporation and, in criminal actions or proceedings, in addition, had no reasonable cause to believe that his conduct was unlawful.

(b) The termination of any such civil or criminal action or proceeding by judgment, settlement, conviction or upon a plea of nolo contendere, or its equivalent, shall not in itself create a presumption that any such director or officer did not act, in good faith, for a purpose which he reasonably believed to be in, or, in the case of service for any other corporation or any partnership, joint venture, trust, employee benefit plan or other enterprise, not opposed to, the best interests of the corporation or that he had reasonable cause to believe that his conduct was unlawful.

(c) For the purpose of this section, a corporation shall be deemed to have requested a person to serve an employee benefit plan where the performance by such person of his duties to the corporation also imposes duties on, or otherwise involves services by, such person to the plan or participants or beneficiaries of the plan; excise taxes assessed on a person with respect to an employee benefit plan pursuant to applicable law shall be considered fines; and action taken or omitted by a person with respect to an employee benefit plan in the performance of such person's duties for a purpose reasonably believed by such person to be in the interest of the participants and beneficiaries of the plan shall be deemed to be for a purpose which is not opposed to the best interests of the corporation.

§ 724. Payment of indemnification other than by court award

(a) A person who has been wholly successful, on the merits or otherwise, in the defense of a civil or criminal action or proceeding of the character described in section 722 (Authorization for indemnification of directors and officers in actions by or in the right of a corporation to procure a judgment in its favor) or 723 (Authorization for indemnification of directors and officers in actions or proceedings other than by or in the right of a corporation to procure a judgment in its favor) shall be entitled to indemnification as authorized in such sections.

(b) Except as provided in paragraph (a), any indemnification under section 722 or 723, unless ordered by a court under section 725 (Indemnification of directors and officers by a court), shall be made by the corporation, only if authorized in the specific case:

(1) By the board acting by a quorum consisting of directors who are not parties to such action or proceeding upon a finding that the director or officer has met the standard of conduct set forth in section 722 or 723, as the case may be, or,

(2) If a quorum under subparagraph (1) is not obtainable with due diligence;

(A) By the board upon the opinion in writing of independent legal counsel that indemnification is proper in the circumstances because the applicable standard of conduct set forth in such sections has been met by such director or officer, or

(B) By the shareholders upon a finding that the director or officer has met the applicable standard of conduct set forth in such sections.

(c) Expenses incurred in defending a civil or criminal action or proceeding may be paid by the corporation in advance of the final disposition of such action or proceeding if authorized under paragraph (b).

§ 725. Indemnification of directors and officers by a court

(a) Notwithstanding the failure of a corporation to provide indemnification, and despite any contrary resolution of the board or of the shareholders in the specific case under section 724 (Payment of indemnification other than by court award), indemnification shall be awarded by a court to the extent authorized under sections 722 (Authorization for indemnification of directors and officers in actions by or in the right of a corporation to procure a judgment in its favor), 723 (Authorization for indemnification of directors and officers in actions or proceedings other than by or in the right of a corporation to procure a judgment in its favor), and paragraph (a) of section 724. Application therefor may be made, in every case, either:

(1) In the civil action or proceeding in which the expenses were incurred or other amounts were paid, or

(2) To the supreme court in a separate proceeding, in which case the application shall set forth the disposition of any previous application made to any court for the same or similar relief and also reasonable cause for the failure to make application for such relief in the action or proceeding in which the expenses were incurred or other amounts were paid.

(b) The application shall be made in such manner and form as may be required by the applicable rules of court or, in the absence thereof, by direction of a court to which it is made. Such application shall be upon notice to the corporation. The court may also direct that notice be given at the expense of the corporation to the shareholders and such other persons as it may designate in such manner as it may require.

(c) Where indemnification is sought by judicial action, the court may allow a person such reasonable expenses, including attorneys' fees, during the pendency of the litigation as are necessary in connection with his defense therein, if the court shall find that the defendant has by his pleadings or during the course of the litigation raised genuine issues of fact or law.

§ 726. Other provisions affecting indemnification of directors and officers

(a) All expenses incurred in defending a civil or criminal action or proceeding which are advanced by the corporation under paragraph (c) of section 724 (Payment of indemnification other than by court award) or allowed by a court under paragraph (c) of section 725 (Indemnification of directors and officers by a court) shall be repaid in case the person receiving such advancement or allowance is ultimately found, under the procedure set forth in this article, not to be entitled to indemnification or, where indemnification is granted, to the extent the expenses so advanced by the corporation or allowed by the court exceed the indemnification to which he is entitled.

(b) No indemnification, advancement or allowance shall be made under this article in any circumstance where it appears:

(1) That the indemnification would be inconsistent with the law of the jurisdiction of incorporation of a foreign corporation which prohibits or otherwise limits such indemnification;

(2) That the indemnification would be inconsistent with a provision of the certificate of incorporation, a by-law, a resolution of the board or of the shareholders, an agreement or other proper corporate action, in effect at the time of the accrual of the alleged cause of action asserted in the threatened or pending action or proceeding in which the expenses were incurred or other amounts were paid, which prohibits or otherwise limits indemnification; or

(3) If there has been a settlement approved by the court, that the indemnification would be inconsistent with any condition with respect to indemnification expressly imposed by the court in approving the settlement.

(c) If, under this article, any expenses or other amounts are paid by way of indemnification, otherwise than by court order or action by the shareholders, the corporation shall, not later than the next annual meeting of shareholders unless such meeting is held within three months from the date of such payment, and, in any event, within fifteen months from the date of such payment, mail to its shareholders of record at the time entitled to vote for the election of directors a statement specifying the persons paid, the amounts paid, and the nature and status at the time of such payment of the litigation or threatened litigation.

.   .   .

§ 727. Insurance for indemnification of directors and officers

(a) Subject to paragraph (b), a corporation shall have power to purchase and maintain insurance:

(1) To indemnify the corporation for any obligation which it incurs as a result of the indemnification of directors and officers under the provisions of this article, and

(2) To indemnify directors and officers in instances in which they may be indemnified by the corporation under the provisions of this article, and

(3) To indemnify directors and officers in instances in which they may not otherwise be indemnified by the corporation under the provisions of this article provided the contract of insurance covering such directors and officers provides, in a manner acceptable to the superintendent of insurance, for a retention amount and for co-insurance.

(b) No insurance under paragraph (a) may provide for any payment, other than cost of defense, to or on behalf of any director or officer.

(1) if a judgment or other final adjudication adverse to the insured director or officer establishes that his acts of active and deliberate dishonesty were material to the cause of action so adjudicated, or that he personally gained in fact a financial profit or other advantage to which he was not legally entitled, or

(2) in relation to any risk the insurance of which is prohibited under the insurance law of this state.

(c) Insurance under any or all subparagraphs of paragraph (a) may be included in a single contract or supplement thereto. Retrospective rated contracts are prohibited.

(d) The corporation shall, within the time and to the persons provided in paragraph (c) of section 726 (Other provisions affecting indemnification of directors or officers), mail a statement in respect of any insurance it has purchased or renewed under this section, specifying the insurance carrier, date of the contract, cost of the insurance, corporate positions insured, and a statement explaining all sums, not previously reported in a statement to shareholders, paid under any indemnification insurance contract.

(e) This section is the public policy of this state to spread the risk of corporate management, notwithstanding any other general or special law of this state or of any other jurisdiction including the federal government.

D. SELECTED CALIFORNIA STATUTES

CORPORATIONS CODE

§ 317. Indemnification of agent of corporation in proceedings or actions

(a) For the purposes of this section, "agent" means any person who is or was a director, officer, employee or other agent of the corporation, or is or was serving at the request of the corporation as a director, officer, employee or agent of another foreign or domestic corporation, partnership, joint venture, trust or other enterprise, or was a director, officer, employee or agent of a foreign or domestic corporation which was a predecessor corporation of the corporation or of another enterprise at the request of such predecessor corporation; "proceeding" means any threatened, pending or completed action or proceeding, whether civil, criminal, administrative or investigative; and "expenses" includes without limitation attorneys' fees and any expenses of establishing a right to indemnification under subdivision (d) or paragraph (3) of subdivision (e).

(b) A corporation shall have power to indemnify any person who was or is a party or is threatened to be made a party to any proceeding (other than an action by or in the right of the corporation to procure a judgment in its favor) by reason of the fact that such person is or was an agent of the corporation, against expenses, judgments, fines, settlements and other amounts actually and reasonably incurred in connection with such proceeding if such person acted in good faith and in a manner such person reasonably believed to be in the best interests of the corporation and, in the case of a criminal proceeding, had no reasonable cause to believe the conduct of such person was unlawful. The termination of any proceeding by judgment, order, settlement, conviction or upon a plea of nolo contendere or its equivalent shall not, of itself, create a presumption that the person did not act in good faith and in a manner which the person reasonably believed to be in the best interests of the corporation or that the person had reasonable cause to believe that the person's conduct was unlawful.

(c) A corporation shall have power to indemnify any person who was or is a party or is threatened to be made a party to any threatened, pending or completed action by or in the right of the corporation to procure a judgment in its favor by reason of the fact that such person is or was an agent of the corporation, against expenses actually and reasonably incurred by such person in connection with the defense or settlement of such action if such person acted in good faith, in a manner such person believed to be in the best interests of the corporation and with such care, including reasonable inquiry, as an ordinarily prudent person in a like position would use under similar circumstances. No indemnification shall be made under this subdivision (c):

(1) In respect of any claim, issue or matter as to which such person shall have been adjudged to be liable to the corporation in the performance of such person's duty to the corporation, unless and only to the extent that the court in which such proceeding is or was pending shall determine upon application that, in view of all the circumstances of the case, such person is fairly and reasonably entitled to indemnity for the expenses which such court shall determine;

(2) Of amounts paid in settling or otherwise disposing of a threatened or pending action, with or without court approval; or

(3) Of expenses incurred in defending a threatened or pending action which is settled or otherwise disposed of without court approval.

(d) To the extent that an agent of a corporation has been successful on the merits in defense of any proceeding referred to in subdivision (b) or (c) or in defense of any claim, issue or matter therein, the agent shall be indemnified against expenses actually and reasonably incurred by the agent in connection therewith.

(e) Except as provided in subdivision (d), any indemnification under this section shall be made by the corporation only if authorized in the specific case, upon a determination that indemnification of the agent is proper in the circumstances because the agent has met the applicable standard of conduct set forth in subdivision (b) or (c), by:

(1) A majority vote of a quorum consisting of directors who are not parties to such proceeding;

(2) Approval of the shareholders (Section 153), with the shares owned by the person to be indemnified not being entitled to vote thereon; or

(3) The court in which such proceeding is or was pending upon application made by the corporation or the agent or the attorney or other person rendering services in connection with the defense, whether or not such application by the agent, attorney or other person is opposed by the corporation.

(f) Expenses incurred in defending any proceeding may be advanced by the corporation prior to the final disposition of such proceeding upon receipt of an undertaking by or on behalf of the agent to repay such amount unless it shall be determined ultimately that the agent is entitled to be indemnified as authorized in this section.

(g) No provision made by a corporation to indemnify its or its subsidiary's directors or officers for the defense of any proceeding, whether contained in the articles, bylaws, a resolution of shareholders or directors, an agreement or otherwise, shall be valid unless consistent with this section. Nothing contained in this section shall affect any right to indemnification to which persons other than such directors and officers may be entitled by contract or otherwise.

(h) No indemnification or advance shall be made under this section, except as provided in subdivision (d) or paragraph (3) of subdivision (e), in any circumstance where it appears:

(1) That it would be inconsistent with a provision of the articles, bylaws, a resolution of the shareholders or an agreement in effect at the time of the accrual of the alleged cause of action asserted in the proceeding in which the expenses were incurred or other amounts were paid, which prohibits or otherwise limits indemnification; or

(2) That it would be inconsistent with any condition expressly imposed by a court in approving a settlement.

(i) A corporation shall have power to purchase and maintain insurance on behalf of any agent of the corporation against any liability asserted against or incurred by the agent in such capacity or arising out of the agent's status as such whether or not the corporation would have the power to indemnify the agent against such liability under the provisions of this section.

(j) This section does not apply to any proceeding against any trustee, investment manager or other fiduciary of an employee benefit plan in such person's capacity as such, even though such person may also be an agent as defined in subdivision (a) of the employer corporation. A corporation shall have the power to indemnify such a trustee, investment manager or other fiduciary to the extent permitted by subdivision (f) of Section 207.

§ 800. Conditions; security; motion for order; determination

(a) As used in this section, "corporation" includes an unincorporated association; "board" includes the managing body of an unincorporated association; "shareholder" includes a member of an unincorporated association; and "shares" includes memberships in an unincorporated association.

(b) No action may be instituted or maintained in right of any domestic or foreign corporation by any holder of shares or of voting trust certificates of such corporation unless both of the following conditions exist:

(1) The plaintiff alleges in the complaint that plaintiff was a shareholder, of record or beneficially, or the holder of voting trust certificates at the time of the transaction or any part thereof of which plaintiff complains or that plaintiff's shares or voting trust certificates thereafter devolved upon plaintiff by operation of law from a holder who was a holder at the time of the transaction or any part thereof complained of; provided, that any shareholder who does not meet such requirements may nevertheless be allowed in the discretion of the court to maintain such action on a preliminary showing to and determination by the court, by motion and after a hearing, at which the court shall consider such evidence, by affidavit or testimony, as it deems material, that (i) there is a strong prima facie case in favor of the claim asserted on behalf of the corporation, (ii) no other similar action has been or is likely to be instituted, (iii) the plaintiff acquired the shares before there was disclosure to the public or to the plaintiff of the wrongdoing of which plaintiff complains, (iv) unless the action can be maintained the defendant may retain a gain derived from defendant's willful breach of a fiduciary duty, and (v) the requested relief will not result in unjust enrichment of the corporation or any shareholder of the corporation; and

(2) The plaintiff alleges in the complaint with particularity plaintiff's efforts to secure from the board such action as plaintiff desires, or the reasons for not making such effort, and alleges further that plaintiff has either informed the corporation or the board in writing of the ultimate facts of each cause of action against each defendant or delivered to the corporation or the board a true copy of the complaint which plaintiff proposes to file.

(c) In any action referred to in subdivision (b), at any time within 30 days after service of summons upon the corporation or upon any defendant who is an officer or director of the corporation, or held such office at the time of the acts complained of, the corporation or such defendant may move the court for an order, upon notice and hearing, requiring the plaintiff to furnish security as hereinafter provided. The motion shall be based upon one or both of the following grounds:

(1) That there is no reasonable possibility that the prosecution of the cause of action alleged in the complaint against the moving party will benefit the corporation or its shareholders.

(2) That the moving party, if other than the corporation, did not participate in the transaction complained of in any capacity.

The court on application of the corporation or any defendant may, for good cause shown, extend the 30-day period for an additional period or periods not exceeding 60 days.

(d) At the hearing upon any motion pursuant to subdivision (c), the court shall consider such evidence, written or oral, by witnesses or affidavit, as may be material (1) to the ground or grounds upon which the motion is based, or (2) to a determination of the probable reasonable expenses, including attorneys' fees, of the corporation and the moving party which will be incurred in the defense of the action. If the court determines, after hearing the evidence adduced by the parties, that the moving party has established a probability in support of any of the grounds upon which the motion is based, the court shall fix the nature and amount of security, not to exceed fifty thousand dollars ($50,000), to be furnished by the plaintiff for reasonable expenses, including attorneys' fees, which may be incurred by the moving party and the corporation in connection with the action, including expenses for which the corporation may become liable pursuant to Section 317. A ruling by the court on the motion shall not be a determination of any issue in the action or of the merits thereof. The amount of the security may thereafter be increased or decreased in the discretion of the court upon a showing that the security provided has or may become inadequate or is excessive, but the court may not in any event increase the total amount of the security beyond fifty thousand dollars ($50,000) in the aggregate for all defendants. If the court, upon any such motion, makes a determination that security shall be furnished by the plaintiff as to any one or more defendants, the action shall be dismissed as to such defendant or defendants, unless the security required by the court shall have been furnished within such reasonable time as may be fixed by the court. The corporation and the moving party shall have recourse to the security in such amount as the court shall determine upon the termination of the action.

(e) If the plaintiff shall, either before or after a motion is made pursuant to subdivision (c), or any order or determination pursuant to such motion, post good and sufficient bond or bonds in the aggregate amount of fifty thousand dollars ($50,000) to secure the reasonable expenses of the parties entitled to make the motion, the plaintiff has complied with the requirements of this section and with any order for security theretofore made pursuant hereto, and any such motion then pending shall be dismissed and no further or additional bond or other security shall be required.

(f) If a motion is filed pursuant to subdivision (c), no pleadings need be filed by the corporation or any other defendant and the prosecution of the action shall be stayed until 10 days after the motion has been disposed of.

E. CODE OF PROFESSIONAL RESPONSIBILITY

(The following excerpts reflect the status of the Code with relevant amendments. "The Code is designed to be adopted by appropriate agencies both as an inspirational guide to the members of the profession and as a basis for disciplinary action when the conduct of a lawyer falls below the required minimum standards stated in the Disciplinary Rules." As of early 1983, a new set of Model Rules of Professional Conduct was in advanced stages of debate within the American Bar Association. It appears that some time may elapse before it becomes generally incorporated into state rules and that it may be further amended before that occurs. One portion of the draft as it stood in December 1982, Rule 1.13 ["Organization as a Client"], seems of such importance to the subject matter of this course that it is included immediately following EC 5–18, which represents the present Code's treatment of that question.)

DISCIPLINARY RULES

DR 4–101   Preservation of Confidences and Secrets of a Client.

(A) "Confidence" refers to information protected by the attorney-client privilege under applicable law, and "secret" refers to other information gained in the professional relationship that the client has requested be held inviolate or the disclosure of which would be embarrassing or would be likely to be detrimental to the client.

(B) Except when permitted under DR 4–101(C), a lawyer shall not knowingly:

  (1) Reveal a confidence or secret of his client.

  (2) Use a confidence or secret of his client to the disadvantage of the client.

  (3) Use a confidence or secret of his client for the advantage of himself or of a third person, unless the client consents after full disclosure.

(C) A lawyer may reveal:

  (1) Confidences or secrets with the consent of the client or clients affected, but only after a full disclosure to them.

  (2) Confidences or secrets when permitted under Disciplinary Rules or required by law or court order.

  (3) The intention of his client to commit a crime and the information necessary to prevent the crime.

  (4) Confidences or secrets necessary to establish or collect his fee or to defend himself or his employees or associates against an accusation of wrongful conduct.

(D) A lawyer shall exercise reasonable care to prevent his employees, associates, and others whose services are utilized by him from disclosing or using confidences or secrets of a client, except that a lawyer may reveal the information allowed by DR 4–101(C) through an employee.

EC 5–18 A lawyer employed or retained by a corporation or similar entity owes his allegiance to the entity and not to a stockholder, director, officer, employee, representative, or other person connected with the entity. In advising the entity, a lawyer should keep paramount its interests and his professional judgment should not be influenced by the personal desires of any person or organization. Occasionally a lawyer for an entity is requested by a stockholder, director, officer, employee, representative, or other person connected with the entity to represent him in an individual capacity; in such case the lawyer may serve the individual only if the lawyer is convinced that differing interests are not present.

[MODEL RULES OF PROFESSIONAL CONDUCT
(IN 1982 FORMAT)]

Rule 1.13   Organization as the Client
(a) A lawyer employed or retained to represent an organization represents the organization as distinct from its directors, officers, employees, members, shareholders or other constituents.
(b) If a lawyer for an organization knows that an officer, employee or other other person associated with the organization is engaged in action, intends to act or refuses to act in a matter related to the representation that is a violation of a legal obligation to the organization, or a violation of law which reasonably might be imputed to the organization, and is likely to result in substantial injury to the organization, the lawyer shall proceed as is reasonably necessary in the best interest of the organization. In determining how to proceed, the lawyer shall give due consideration to the seriousness of the violation and its consequences, the scope and nature of the lawyer's representation, the responsibility in the organization and the apparent motivation of the person involved, the policies of the organization concerning such matters and any other relevant considerations. Any measures taken shall be designed to minimize disruption of the organization and the risk of revealing information relating to the representation to persons outside the organization. Such measures may include among others:
(1) asking reconsideration of the matter;
(2) advising that a separate legal opinion on the matter be sought for presentation to appropriate authority in the organization; and
(3) referring the matter to higher authority in the organization, including, if warranted by the seriousness of the matter, referral to the highest authority that can act in behalf of the organization as determined by applicable law.
(c) When the organization's highest authority insists upon action, or refuses to take action, that is clearly a violation of a legal obligation to the organization, or a violation of law which reasonably might be imputed to the organization, and is likely to result in substantial injury to the organization, the lawyer may take further remedial action that the lawyer reasonably believes to be in the best interest of the organ-

ization. Such action may include revealing information otherwise protected by Rule 1.6 only if the lawyer reasonably believes that:

(1) the highest authority in the organization has acted to further the personal or financial interests of members of that authority which are in conflict with the interests of the organization; and

(2) revealing the information is necessary in the best interest of the organization.

(d) In dealing with an organization's directors, officers, employees, members, shareholders or other constituents, a lawyer shall explain the identity of the client when the lawyer believes that such explanation is necessary to avoid misunderstandings on their part.

(e) A lawyer representing an organization may also represent any of its directors, officers, employees, members, shareholders or other constituents, subject to the provisions of Rule 1.7. If the organization's consent to the dual representation is required by Rule 1.7, the consent shall be given by an appropriate official of the organization other than the individual who is to be represented or by the shareholders.]

DR 5–101   Refusing Employment When the Interests of the Lawyer May Impair His Independent Professional Judgment.

(A) Except with the consent of his client after full disclosure, a lawyer shall not accept employment if the exercise of his professional judgment on behalf of his client will be or reasonably may be affected by his own financial, business, property, or personal interests.

(B) A lawyer shall not accept employment in contemplated or pending litigation if he knows or it is obvious that he or a lawyer in his firm ought to be called as a witness, except that he may undertake the employment and he or a lawyer in his firm may testify:

(1) If the testimony will relate solely to an uncontested matter.

(2) If the testimony will relate solely to a matter of formality and there is no reason to believe that substantial evidence will be offered in opposition to the testimony.

(3) If the testimony will relate solely to the nature and value of legal services rendered in the case by the lawyer or his firm to the client.

(4) As to any matter, if refusal would work a substantial hardship on the client because of the distinctive value of the lawyer or his firm as counsel in the particular case.

DR 5–104   Limiting Business Relations with a Client.

(A) A lawyer shall not enter into a business transaction with a client if they have differing interests therein and if the client expects the lawyer to exercise his professional judgment therein for the protection of the client, unless the client has consented after full disclosure.

(B) Prior to conclusion of all aspects of the matter giving rise to his employment, a lawyer shall not enter into any arrangement or understanding with a client or a prospective client by which he acquires an interest in publication rights with respect to the subject matter of his employment or proposed employment.

DR 5–105　Refusing to Accept or Continue Employment if the Interests of Another Client May Impair the Independent Professional Judgment of the Lawyer.

(A) A lawyer shall decline proffered employment if the exercise of his independent professional judgment in behalf of a client will be or is likely to be adversely affected by the acceptance of the proffered employment, or if it would be likely to involve him in representing differing interests, except to the extent permitted under DR 5–105(C).

(B) A lawyer shall not continue multiple employment if the exercise of his independent professional judgment in behalf of a client will be or is likely to be adversely affected by his representation of another client, or if it would be likely to involve him in representing differing interests, except to the extent permitted under DR 5–105(C).

(C) In the situations covered by DR 5–105(A) and (B), a lawyer may represent multiple clients if it is obvious that he can adequately represent the interest of each and if each consents to the representation after full disclosure of the possible effect of such representation on the exercise of his independent professional judgment on behalf of each.

(D) If a lawyer is required to decline employment or to withdraw from employment under a Disciplinary Rule, no partner, or associate, or any other lawyer affiliated with him or his firm, may accept or continue such employment.

DR 5–107　Avoiding Influence by Others Than the Client.

(A) Except with the consent of his client after full disclosure, a lawyer shall not:

(1) Accept compensation for his legal services from one other than his client.

(2) Accept from one other than his client any thing of value related to his representation of or his employment by his client.

(B) A lawyer shall not permit a person who recommends, employs, or pays him to render legal services for another to direct or regulate his professional judgment in rendering such legal services.

(C) A lawyer shall not practice with or in the form of a professional corporation or association authorized to practice law for a profit, if:

(1) A non-lawyer owns any interest therein, except that a fiduciary representative of the estate of a lawyer may hold the stock or interest of the lawyer for a reasonable time during administration;

(2) A non-lawyer is a corporate director or officer thereof; or

(3) A non-lawyer has the right to direct or control the professional judgment of a lawyer.

DR 7–101 Representing a Client Zealously.

(A) A lawyer shall not intentionally:

(1) Fail to seek the lawful objectives of his client through reasonably available means permitted by law and the Disciplinary Rules, except as provided by DR 7–101(B). A lawyer does not violate this Disciplinary Rule, however, by acceding to reasonable requests of opposing counsel which do not prejudice the rights of his client, by being punctual in fulfilling all professional commitments, by avoiding offensive tactics, or by treating with courtesy and consideration all persons involved in the legal process.

(2) Fail to carry out a contract of employment entered into with a client for professional services, but he may withdraw as permitted under DR 2–110, DR 5–102, and DR 5–105.

(3) Prejudice or damage his client during the course of the professional relationship, except as required under DR 7–102(B).

(B) In his representation of a client, a lawyer may:

(1) Where permissible, exercise his professional judgment to waive or fail to assert a right or position of his client.

(2) Refuse to aid or participate in conduct that he believes to be unlawful, even though there is some support for an argument that the conduct is legal.

DR 7–102 Representing a Client Within the Bounds of the Law.

(A) In his representation of a client, a lawyer shall not:

(1) File a suit, assert a position, conduct a defense, delay a trial, or take other action on behalf of his client when he knows or when it is obvious that such action would serve merely to harass or maliciously injure another.

(2) Knowingly advance a claim or defense that is unwarranted under existing law, except that he may advance such claim or defense if it can be supported by good faith argument for an extension, modification, or reversal of existing law.

(3) Conceal or knowingly fail to disclose that which he is required by law to reveal.

(4) Knowingly use perjured testimony or false evidence.

(5) Knowingly make a false statement of law or fact.

(6) Participate in the creation or preservation of evidence when he knows or it is obvious that the evidence is false.

(7) Counsel or assist his client in conduct that the lawyer knows to be illegal or fraudulent.

(8) Knowingly engage in other illegal conduct or conduct contrary to a Disciplinary Rule.

(B) A lawyer who receives information clearly establishing that:

    (1) His client has, in the course of the representation, perpetrated a fraud upon a person or tribunal shall promptly call upon his client to rectify the same, and if his client refuses or is unable to do so, he shall reveal the fraud to the affected person or tribunal, except when the information is protected as a privileged communication.

    (2) A person other than his client has perpetrated a fraud upon a tribunal shall promptly reveal the fraud to the tribunal.

B. RECENT CASES

Chapter X

SHAREHOLDERS' DERIVATIVE SUITS

ZAPATA CORP. v. MALDONADO

Supreme Court of Delaware, 1981.
430 A.2d 779.

[In 1975 Maldonado, a stockholder of Zapata, began a derivative suit in the Delaware Court of Chancery charging ten of its officers and directors with breaches of fiduciary duty. He stated that a demand would be futile as all directors were defendants. In 1977 he began a parallel suit in the U. S. District Court for the Southern District of New York. Another shareholder sued in Texas. By 1979 Zapata's board had changed membership and it appointed an "Independent Investigation Committee" composed of two new directors to investigate this litigation. In September 1979 the Committee reported that the actions should "be dismissed forthwith as their continued maintenance is inimical to the Company's best interests . . . ." The New York federal district court granted a summary judgment motion on January 24, 1980 as did the one in Texas. On March 18, 1980 the Court of Chancery denied a like motion. The Court of Appeals for the Second Circuit stayed the appeal before it pending a Delaware ruling. On May 29th the Chancery Court dismissed the suit on the ground that the federal disposition was res judicata—if sustained on appeal. However, the United States Court of Appeals for the Second Circuit ordered the federal appeal stayed pending the Delaware Supreme Court's disposition of the state appeal. Thus the litigation sat "in a procedural gridlock." The Delaware Supreme Court accepted an interlocutory appeal. It reversed the Court of Chancery and remanded for further proceedings on an opinion by JUSTICE QUILLEN.]

Thus, Zapata's observation that it sits "in a procedural gridlock" appears quite accurate, and we agree that this Court can and should attempt to resolve the particular question of Delaware law. As the Vice Chancellor noted, 413 A.2d at 1257, "it is the law of the State of incorporation which determines whether the directors have this power of dismissal. Burks v. Lasker, 441 U.S. 471, 99 S.Ct. 1831, 60 L.Ed.2d 404 (1979)". We limit our review in this interlocutory appeal to whether the Committee has the power to cause the present action to be dismissed.

We begin with an examination of the carefully considered opinion of the Vice Chancellor which states, in part, that the "business judgment" rule does not confer power "to a corporate board of directors to terminate a derivative suit", 413 A.2d at 1257. His conclusion is particularly pertinent because several federal courts, applying Delaware law, have held that the

116

business judgment rule enables boards (or their committees) to terminate derivative suits, decisions now in conflict with the holding below.

As the term is most commonly used, and given the disposition below, we can understand the Vice Chancellor's comment that "the business judgment rule is irrelevant to the question of whether the Committee has the authority to compel the dismissal of this suit". 413 A.2d at 1257. Corporations, existing because of legislative grace, possess authority as granted by the legislature. Directors of Delaware corporations derive their managerial decision making power, which encompasses decisions whether to initiate, or refrain from entering, litigation, from 8 Del.C. § 141(a). This statute is the fount of directorial powers. The "business judgment" rule is a judicial creation that presumes propriety, under certain circumstances, in a board's decision. Viewed defensively, it does not create authority. In this sense the "business judgment" rule is not relevant in corporate decision making until after a decision is made. It is generally used as a defense to an attack on the decision's soundness. The board's managerial decision making power, however, comes from § 141(a). The judicial creation and legislative grant are related because the "business judgment" rule evolved to give recognition and deference to directors' business expertise when exercising their managerial power under § 141(a).

In the case before us, although the corporation's decision to move to dismiss or for summary judgment was, literally, a decision resulting from an exercise of the directors' (as delegated to the Committee) business judgment, the question of "business judgment", in a defensive sense, would not become relevant until and unless the decision to seek termination of the derivative lawsuit was attacked as improper . . .   This question was not reached by the Vice Chancellor because he determined that the stockholder had an individual right to maintain this derivative action. *Maldonado*, 413 A.2d at 1262.

Thus, the focus in this case is on the power to speak for the corporation as to whether the lawsuit should be continued or terminated. As we see it, this issue in the current appellate posture of this case has three aspects: the conclusions of the Court below concerning the continuing right of a stockholder to maintain a derivative action; the corporate power under Delaware law of an authorized board committee to cause dismissal of litigation instituted for the benefit of the corporation; and the role of the Court of Chancery in resolving conflicts between the stockholder and the committee.

Accordingly, we turn first to the Court of Chancery's conclusions concerning the right of a plaintiff stockholder in a derivative action. We find that its determination that a stockholder, once demand is made and refused, possesses an independent, individual right to continue a derivative suit for breaches of fiduciary duty over objection by the corporation, *Maldonado*, 413 A.2d at 1262–63, as an absolute rule, is erroneous. The Court of Chancery relied principally upon Sohland v. Baker, Del.Supr., 141 A. 277 (1927), for this statement of the Delaware rule. *Maldonado*, 413 A.2d at 1260–61. *Sohland* is sound law. But *Sohland* cannot be fairly read as supporting the broad proposition which evolved in the opinion below.

In *Sohland*, the complaining stockholder was allowed to file the derivative action in equity after making demand and after the board refused to bring the lawsuit. But the question before us relates to the power of the corporation by motion to terminate a lawsuit properly commenced by a stockholder without prior demand. No Delaware statute or case cited to us directly determines this new question and we do not think that *Sohland* addresses it by implication. . . .

Moreover, McKee v. Rogers, Del.Ch., 156 A. 191 (1931), stated "as a general rule" that "a stockholder cannot be permitted . . . to invade the discretionary field committed to the judgment of the directors and sue in the corporation's behalf when the managing body refuses. This rule is a well settled one." 156 A. at 193.[9]

The *McKee* rule, of course, should not be read so broadly that the board's refusal will be determinative in every instance. Board members, owing a well-established fiduciary duty to the corporation, will not be allowed to cause a derivative suit to be dismissed when it would be a breach of their fiduciary duty. Generally disputes pertaining to control of the suit arise in two contexts.

Consistent with the purpose of requiring a demand, a board decision to cause a derivative suit to be dismissed as detrimental to the company, after demand has been made and refused, will be respected unless it was wrongful.[10] . . . A claim of a wrongful decision not to sue is thus the first exception and the first context of dispute. Absent a wrongful refusal, the stockholder in such a situation simply lacks legal managerial power. Compare *Maldonado*, 413 A.2d at 1259–60.

But it cannot be implied that, absent a wrongful board refusal, a stockholder can never have an individual right to initiate an action. For, as is stated in *McKee*, a "well settled" exception exists to the general rule.

> "[A] stockholder may sue in equity in his derivative right to assert a cause of action in behalf of the corporation, *without prior demand* upon the directors to sue, when it is apparent that a demand would be futile, that the officers are under an influence that sterilizes discretion and could not be proper persons to conduct the litigation."

156 A. at 193 (emphasis added). This exception, the second context for dispute, is consistent with the Court of Chancery's statement below, that "[t]he

---

9. To the extent that Mayer v. Adams, Del.Supr., 141 A.2d 458, 462 (1958) and Ainscow v. Sanitary Co. of America, Del.Ch., 180 A. 614, 615 (1935) relied upon in *Maldonado*, 413 A.2d at 1262, contained language relating to the rule in *McKee*, we note that each decision is dissimilar from the one we examine today. *Mayer* held that demand on the stockholders was not required before maintaining a derivative suit if the wrong alleged could not be ratified by the stockholders. *Ainscow* found defective a compliant that neither alleged demand on the directors, nor reasons why demand was excusable.

10. In other words, when stockholders, after making demand and having their

suit rejected, attack the board's decision as improper, the board's decision falls under the "business judgment" rule and will be respected if the requirements of the rule are met. See Dent, supra note 5, 75 Nw.U.L.Rev. at 100–01 & nn. 24–25. That situation should be distinguished from the instant case, where demand was not made, and the *power* of the board to seek a dismissal, due to disqualification, presents a threshold issue. For examples of what has been held to be a wrongful decision not to sue, see Stockholder Derivative Actions, supra note 5, 44 U.Chi.L.Rev. at 193–98. We recognize that the two contexts can overlap in practice.

stockholders' individual right to bring the action does not ripen, however, . . . unless he can show a demand to be futile." *Maldonado*, 413 A.2d at 1262.[11]

These comments in *McKee* and in the opinion below make obvious sense. A demand, when required and refused (if not wrongful), terminates a stockholder's legal ability to initiate a derivative action.[12] But where demand is properly excused, the stockholder does possess the ability to initiate the action on his corporation's behalf.

These conclusions, however, do not determine the question before us. Rather, they merely bring us to the question to be decided. It is here that we part company with the Court below. Derivative suits enforce corporate rights and any recovery obtained goes to the corporation. *Taormina v. Taormina Corp.*, Del.Ch., 78 A.2d 473, 476 (1951); *Keenan v. Eshleman*, Del.Supr., 2 A.2d 904, 912–13 (1938). "The right of a stockholder to file a bill to litigate corporate rights is, therefore, solely for the purpose of preventing injustice where it is apparent that material corporate rights would not otherwise be protected." *Sohland*, 141 A. at 282. We see no inherent reason why the "two phases" of a derivative suit, the stockholder's suit to compel the corporation to sue and the corporation's suit (see 413 A.2d at 1261–62), should automatically result in the placement in the hands of the litigating stockholder sole control of the corporate right throughout the litigation. To the contrary, it seems to us that such an inflexible rule would recognize the interest of one person or group to the exclusion of all others within the corporate entity. Thus, we reject the view of the Vice Chancellor as to the first aspect of the issue on appeal.

The question to be decided becomes: When, if at all, should an authorized board committee be permitted to cause litigation, properly initiated by a derivative stockholder in his own right, to be dismissed? As noted above, a board has the power to choose not to pursue litigation when demand is made upon it, so long as the decision is not wrongful. If the board determines that a suit would be detrimental to the company, the board's determination prevails. Even when demand is excusable, circumstances may arise when continuation of the litigation would not be in the corporation's best interests. Our inquiry is whether, under such circumstances, there is a permissible procedure under § 141(a) by which a corporation can rid itself of detrimental litigation. If there is not, a single stockholder in an extreme case might control the destiny of the entire corporation. This concern was bluntly expressed by the Ninth Circuit in *Lewis v. Anderson*, 9th Cir., 615 F.2d 778, 783 (1979), cert. denied, 449 U.S. 869, 101 S.Ct. 206, 66 L.Ed.2d 89 (1980): "To allow one shareholder to incapacitate an entire board of directors merely by leveling charges against them gives too much leverage to dissident shareholders." But, when examining the means, including the

---

11. These statements are consistent with Rule 23.1's "reasons for . . . failure" to make demand. See also the other cases cited by the Vice Chancellor, 413 A.2d at 1262: Ainscow v. Sanitary Co. of America, supra note 9, 180 A. at 615; Meyer v. Adams, supra note 9, 141 A.2d at 462; Dann v. Chrysler Corp., Del.Ch., 174 A.2d 696, 699–700 (1961).

12. **Even in this situation, it may take litigation to determine the stockholder's lack of power, i.e., standing.**

committee mechanism examined in this case, potentials for abuse must be recognized. This takes us to the second and third aspects of the issue on appeal.

Before we pass to equitable considerations as to the mechanism at issue here, it must be clear that an independent committee possesses the corporate power to seek the termination of a derivative suit. Section 141(c) allows a board to delegate all of its authority to a committee. Accordingly, a committee with properly delegated authority would have the power to move for dismissal or summary judgment if the entire board did.

Even though demand was not made in this case and the initial decision of whether to litigate was not placed before the board, Zapata's board, it seems to us, retained all of its corporate power concerning litigation decisions. If Maldonado had made demand on the board in this case, it could have refused to bring suit. Maldonado could then have asserted that the decision not to sue was wrongful and, if correct, would have been allowed to maintain the suit. The board, however, never would have lost its statutory managerial authority. The demand requirement itself evidences that the managerial power is retained by the board. When a derivative plaintiff is allowed to bring suit after a wrongful refusal, the board's authority to choose whether to pursue the litigation is not challenged although its conclusion—reached through the exercise of that authority—is not respected since it is wrongful. Similarly, Rule 23.1, by excusing demand in certain instances, does not strip the board of its corporate power. It merely saves the plaintiff the expense and delay of making a futile demand resulting in a probable tainted exercise of that authority in a refusal by the board or in giving control of litigation to the opposing side. But the board entity remains empowered under § 141(a) to make decisions regarding corporate litigation. The problem is one of member disqualification, not the absence of power in the board.

The corporate power inquiry then focuses on whether the board, tainted by the self-interest of a majority of its members, can legally delegate its authority to a committee of two disinterested directors. We find our statute clearly requires an affirmative answer to this question. As has been noted, under an express provision of the statute, § 141(c), a committee can exercise all of the authority of the board to the extent provided in the resolution of the board. Moreover, at least by analogy to our statutory section on interested directors, 8 Del.C. § 141, it seems clear that the Delaware statute is designed to permit disinterested directors to act for the board. Compare Puma v. Marriott, Del.Ch., 283 A.2d 693, 695–96 (1971).

We do not think that the interest taint of the board majority is per se a legal bar to the delegation of the board's power to an independent committee composed of disinterested board members. The committee can properly act for the corporation to move to dismiss derivative litigation that is believed to be detrimental to the corporation's best interest.

Our focus now switches to the Court of Chancery which is faced with a stockholder assertion that a derivative suit, properly instituted should continue for the benefit of the corporation and the corporate assertion, properly made by a board committee acting with board authority, that the same derivative suit should be dismised as inimical to the best interests of the corporation.

At the risk of stating the obvious, the problem is relatively simple. If, on the one hand, corporations can consistently wrest bona fide derivative actions away from well-meaning derivative plaintiffs through the use of the committee mechanism, the derivative suit will lose much, if not all, of its generally-recognized effectiveness as an intra-corporate means of policing boards of directors. See Dent, supra note 5, 75 Nw.U.L.Rev. at 96 & n. 3, 144 & n. 241. If, on the other hand, corporations are unable to rid themselves of meritless or harmful litigation and strike suits, the derivative action, created to benefit the corporation, will produce the opposite, unintended result. . . . It thus appears desirable to us to find a balancing point where bona fide stockholder power to bring corporate causes of action cannot be unfairly trampled on by the board of directors, but the corporation can rid itself of detrimental litigation.

As we noted, the question has been treated by other courts as one of the "business judgment" of the board committee. If a "committee, composed of independent and disinterested directors, conducted a proper review of the matters before it, considered a variety of factors and reached, in good faith, a business judgment that [the] action was not in the best interest of [the corporation]", the action must be dismissed. See, e.g., Maldonado v. Flynn, supra, 485 F.Supp. at 282, 286. The issues become solely independence, good faith, and reasonable investigation. The ultimate conclusion of the committee, under that view, is not subject to judicial review.

We are not satisfied, however, that acceptance of the "business judgment" rationale at this stage of derivative litigation is a proper balancing point. While we admit an analogy with a normal case respecting board judgment, it seems to us that there is sufficient risk in the realities of a situation like the one presented in this case to justify caution beyond adherence to the theory of business judgment.

The context here is a suit against directors where demand on the board is excused. We think some tribute must be paid to the fact that the lawsuit was properly initiated. It is not a board refusal case. Moreover, this complaint was filed in June of 1975 and, while the parties undoubtedly would take differing views on the degree of litigation activity, we have to be concerned about the creation of an "Independent Investigation Committee" four years later, after the election of two new outside directors. Situations could develop where such motions could be filed after years of vigorous litigation for reasons unconnected with the merits of the lawsuit.

Moreover, notwithstanding our conviction that Delaware law entrusts the corporate power to a properly authorized committee, we must be mindful that directors are passing judgment on fellow directors in the same corporation and fellow directors, in this instance, who designated them to serve both as directors and committee members. The question naturally arises whether a "there but for the grace of God go I" empathy might not play a role. And the further question arises whether inquiry as to independence, good faith and reasonable investigation is sufficient safeguard against abuse, perhaps subconscious abuse.

There is another line of exploration besides the factual context of this litigation which we find helpful. The nature of this motion finds no ready pigeonhole, as perhaps illustrated by its being set forth in the alternative. It is perhaps best considered as a hybrid summary judgment motion for dismissal because the stockholder plaintiff's standing to maintain the suit has been lost. But it does not fit neatly into a category described in Rule 12(b) of the Court of Chancery Rules nor does it correspond directly with Rule 56 since the question of genuine issues of fact on the merits of the stockholder's claim are not reached.

It seems to us that there are two other procedural analogies that are helpful in addition to reference to Rules 12 and 56. There is some analogy to a settlement in that there is a request to terminate litigation without a judicial determination of the merits. See Perrine v. Pennroad Corp., Del. Supr., 47 A.2d 479, 487 (1946). "In determining whether or not to approve a proposed settlement of a derivative stockholders' action [when directors are on both sides of the transaction], the Court of Chancery is called upon to exercise its own business judgment." Neponsit Investment Co. v. Abramson, Del.Supr., 405 A.2d 97, 100 (1979) and cases therein cited. In this case, the litigating stockholder plaintiff facing dismissal of a lawsuit properly commenced ought, in our judgment, to have sufficient status for strict Court review.

Finally, if the committee is in effect given status to speak for the corporation as the plaintiff in interest, then it seems to us there is an analogy to Court of Chancery Rule 41(a)(2) where the plaintiff seeks a dismissal after an answer. Certainly, the position of record of the litigating stockholder is adverse to the position advocated by the corporation in the motion to dismiss. Accordingly, there is perhaps some wisdom to be gained by the direction in Rule 41(a)(2) that "an action shall not be dismissed at the plaintiff's instance save upon order of the Court and upon such terms and conditions as the Court deems proper."

Whether the Court of Chancery will be persuaded by the exercise of a committee power resulting in a summary motion for dismissal of a derivative action, where a demand has not been initially made, should rest, in our judgment, in the independent discretion of the Court of Chancery. We thus steer a middle course between those cases which yield to the independent business judgment of a board committee and this case as determined below which would yield to unbridled plaintiff stockholder control. In pursuit of the course, we recognize that "[t]he final substantive judgment whether a particular lawsuit should be maintained requires a balance of many factors— ethical, commercial, promotional, public relations, employee relations, fiscal as well as legal." Maldonado v. Flynn, supra, 485 F.Supp. at 285. But we are content that such factors are not "beyond the judicial reach" of the Court of Chancery which regularly and competently deals with fiduciary relationships, disposition of trust property, approval of settlements and scores of similar problems. We recognize the danger of judicial overreaching but the alternatives seem to us to be outweighed by the fresh view of a judicial outsider. Moreover, if we failed to balance all the interests involved, we would in the name of practicality and judicial economy foreclose a judicial decision on the merits. At this point, we are not convinced that is necessary or desirable.

After an objective and thorough investigation of a derivative suit, an independent committee may cause its corporation to file a pretrial motion to dismiss in the Court of Chancery. The basis of the motion is the best interests of the corporation, as determined by the committee. The motion should include a thorough written record of the investigation and its findings and recommendations. Under appropriate Court supervision, akin to proceedings on summary judgment, each side should have an opportunity to make a record on the motion. As to the limited issues presented by the motion noted below, the moving party should be prepared to meet the normal burden under Rule 56 that there is no genuine issue as to any material fact and that the moving party is entitled to dismiss as a matter of law.[15] The Court should apply a two-step test to the motion.

First, the Court should inquire into the independence and good faith of the committee and the bases supporting its conclusions. Limited discovery may be ordered to facilitate such inquiries. The corporation should have the burden of proving independence, good faith and a reasonable investigation, rather than presuming independence, good faith and reasonableness.[17] If the Court determines either that the committee is not independent or has not shown reasonable bases for its conclusions, or, if the Court is not satisfied for other reasons relating to the process, including but not limited to the good faith of the committee, the Court shall deny the corporation's motion. If, however, the Court is satisfied under Rule 56 standards that the committee was independent and showed reasonable bases for good faith findings and recommendations, the Court may proceed, in its discretion, to the next step.

The second step provides, we believe, the essential key in striking the balance between legitimate corporate claims as expressed in a derivative stockholder suit and a corporation's best interests as expressed by an independent investigating committee. The Court should determine, applying its own independent business judgment, whether the motion should be granted. This means, of course, that instances could arise where a committee can establish its independence and sound bases for its good faith decisions and still have the corporation's motion denied. The second step is intended to thwart instances where corporate actions meet the criteria of step one, but the result does not appear to satisfy its spirit, or where corporate actions would simply prematurely terminate a stockholder grievance deserving of further consideration in the corporation's interest. The Court of Chancery of course must carefully consider and weigh how compelling the corporate interest in dismissal is when faced with a non-frivolous lawsuit. The Court of Chan-

15. We do not foreclose a discretionary trial of factual issues but that issue is not presented in this appeal. See Lewis v. Anderson, supra, 615 F.2d at 780. Nor do we foreclose the possibility that other motions may proceed or be joined with such a pretrial summary judgment motion to dismiss, e.g., a partial motion for summary judgment on the merits.

17. Compare Auerbach v. Bennett, 47 N.Y.2d 619, 419 N.Y.S.2d 920, 928–29,

393 N.E.2d 994 (1979). Our approach here is analoguous to and consistent with the Delaware approach to "interested director" transactions, where the directors, once the transaction is attacked, have the burden of establishing its "intrinsic fairness" to a court's careful scrutiny. See, e.g., Sterling v. Mayflower Hotel Corp., Del.Supr., 93 A.2d 107 (1952).

cery should, when appropriate, give special consideration to matters of law and public policy in addition to the corporation's best interests.

If the Court's independent business judgment is satisfied, the Court may proceed to grant the motion, subject, of course, to any equitable terms or conditions the Court finds necessary or desirable.

Chapter XI

TRANSACTIONS IN SECURITIES
ALREADY ISSUED

CHIARELLA v. UNITED STATES

Supreme Court of the United States, 1980.
445 U.S. 222, 100 S.Ct. 1108, 63 L.Ed.2d 348.

[Chiarella was a "markup man" in the composing room of Pandick Press, a New York financial printer. In the course of that work, petitioner handled documents relating to 5 corporate takeover bids. Although the corporate names were left as blanks or aliases until the night of final printing, Chiarella was able to deduce the names. He bought stock in the target companies and sold immediately after the offers became public, thus realizing a gain of $30,000 in 14 months. When the facts came out Pandick discharged Chiarella. The SEC both filed an injunction action (settled by a consent order in which Chiarella agreed to return the gains) and indicted him for violating § 10b, Rule 10b–5 and § 32 which imposes criminal penalties for wilfull violations of the 1934 Act. He was convicted on all counts and the conviction was affirmed by the Court of Appeals. The Supreme Court granted certiorari and reversed with an opinion by MR. JUSTICE POWELL, in part as follows:]

This case concerns the legal effect of the petitioner's silence. The District Court's charge permitted the jury to convict the petitioner if it found that he willfully failed to inform sellers of target company securities that he knew of a forthcoming takeover bid that would make their shares more valuable. In order to decide whether silence in such circumstances violates § 10(b), it is necessary to review the language and legislative history of that statute as well as its interpretation by the Commission and the federal courts.

Although the starting point of our inquiry is the language of the statute, Ernst & Ernst v. Hochfelder, 425 U.S. 185, 197, 96 S.Ct. 1375, 1382, 47 L.Ed. 2d 668 (1976), § 10(b) does not state whether silence may constitute a manipulative or deceptive device. Section 10(b) was designed as a catch-all clause to prevent fraudulent practices. Id., at 202, 206. But neither the legislative history nor the statute itself affords specific guidance for the resolution of this case. When Rule 10b–5 was promulgated in 1942, the SEC did not discuss the possibility that failure to provide information might run afoul of § 10(b).

The SEC took an important step in the development of § 10(b) when it held that a broker-dealer and his firm violated that section by selling securities on the basis of undisclosed information obtained from a director of the issuer corporation who was also a registered representative of the brokerage firm. In Cady, Roberts & Co., 40 S.E.C. 907 (1961), the Commission decided that a corporate insider must abstain from trading in the shares of his corporation unless he has first disclosed all material inside information known to him. The obligation to disclose or abstain derives from "[a]n affirmative duty to disclose material information[,] [which] has been traditionally imposed on corporate 'insiders,' particular officers, directors, or controlling stockholders. We, and the courts have consistently held that insiders must disclose material facts which are known to them by virtue of their position but which are not known to persons with whom they deal and which, if known, would affect their investment judgment." Id., at 911.

The Commission emphasized that the duty arose from (i) The existence of a relationship affording access to inside information intended to be available only for a corporate purpose, and (ii) the unfairness of allowing a corporate insider to take advantage of that information by trading without disclosure. Id., at 912, and n. 15.

That the relationship between a corporate insider and the stockholders of his corporation gives rise to a disclosure obligation is not a novel twist of the law. At common law, misrepresentation made for the purpose of inducing reliance upon the false statement is fraudulent. But one who fails to disclose material information prior to the consummation of a transaction commits fraud only when he is under a duty to do so. And the duty to disclose arises when one party has information "that the other [party] is entitled to know because of a fiduciary or similar relation of trust and confidence between them." In its *Cady, Roberts* decision, the Commission recognized a relationship of trust and confidence between the shareholders of a corporation and those insiders who have obtained confidential information by reason of their position with that corporation. This relationship gives rise to a duty to disclose because of the "necessity of preventing a corporate insider from [taking] . . . unfair advantage of the uninformed minority stockholders." Speed v. Transamerica Corp., 99 F.Supp. 808, 829 (D.Del. 1951).

The Federal courts have found violations of § 10(b) where corporate insiders used undisclosed information for their own benefit. E.g., SEC v. Texas Gulf Sulphur Co., 401 F.2d 833 (CA2 1968), cert. denied, 404 U.S. 1005, 92 S.Ct. 561, 30 L.Ed.2d 558 (1972). The cases also have emphasized, in accordance with the common-law rule, that "[t]he party charged with failing to disclose market information must be under a duty to disclose it." Frigitemp Corp. v. Financial Dynamics Fund, Inc., 524 F.2d 275, 282 (CA2 1975). Accordingly, a purchaser of stock who has no duty to a prospective seller because he is neither an insider nor a fiduciary has been held to have no obligation to reveal material facts. See General Time Corp. v. Talley Industries, Inc., 403 F.2d 159, 164 (CA2 1968), cert. denied, 393 U.S. 1026, 89 S.Ct. 631, 21 L.Ed.2d 570 (1969).

This Court followed the same approach in Affiliated Ute Citizens v. United States, 406 U.S. 128, 92 S.Ct. 1456, 31 L.Ed.2d 741 (1972). A group of American Indians formed a corporation to manage joint assets derived from tribal holdings. The corporation issued stock to its Indian shareholders and designated a local bank as its transfer agent. Because of the speculative nature of the corporate assets and the difficulty of ascertaining the true value of a share, the corporation requested the bank to stress to its stockholders the importance of retaining the stock. Id., at 146, 92 S.Ct., at 1468. Two of the bank's assistant managers aided the shareholders in disposing of stock which the managers knew was traded in two separate markets—a primary market of Indians selling to non-Indians through the bank and a resale market consisting entirely of non-Indians. Indian sellers charged that the assistant managers had violated § 10(b) and Rule 10b–5 by failing to inform them of the higher prices prevailing in the resale market. The Court recognized that no duty of disclosure would exist if the bank merely had acted as a transfer agent. But the bank also had assumed a duty to act on behalf of the shareholders, and the Indian sellers had relied upon its personnel when they sold their stock. Id., at 152, 92 S.Ct., at 1471. Because these officers of the bank were charged with a responsibility to the shareholders, they could not act as market makers inducing the Indians to sell their stock without disclosing the existence of the more favorable non-Indian market. Id., at 152–153, 92 S.Ct., at 1471–1472.

Thus, administrative and judicial interpretations have established that silence in connection with the purchase or sale of securities may operate as a fraud actionable under § 10(b) despite the absence of statutory language or legislative history specifically addressing the legality of nondisclosure. But such liability is premised upon a duty to disclose arising from a relationship of trust and confidence between parties to a transaction. Application of a duty to disclose prior to trading guarantees that corporate insiders, who have an obligation to place the shareholder's welfare before their own, will not benefit personally through fraudulent use of material nonpublic information.

III

In this case, the petitioner was convicted of violating § 10(b) although he was not a corporate insider and he received no confidential information from the target company. Moreover, the "market information" upon which he relied did not concern the earning power or operations of the target company, but only the plans of the acquiring company. Petitioner's use of that information was not a fraud under § 10(b) unless he was subject to an affirmative duty to disclose it before trading. In this case, the jury instructions failed to specify any such duty. In effect, the trial court instructed the jury that petitioner owed a duty to everyone; to all sellers, indeed, to the market as a whole. The jury simply was told to decide whether petitioner used material, nonpublic information at a time when "he knew other people trading in the securities market did not have access to the same information." Record, at 677.

The Court of Appeals affirmed the conviction by holding that "[a]nyone—corporate insider or not—who regularly receives material nonpublic information may not use that information to trade in securities without incurring an affirmative duty to disclose." 588 F.2d 1358, 1365 (CA2 1978) (emphasis in original). Although the court said that its test would include only persons who regularly receive material nonpublic information, id., at 1366, its rationale for that limitation is unrelated to the existence of a duty to disclose. The Court of Appeals, like the trial court, failed to identify a relationship between petitioner and the sellers that could give rise to a duty. Its decision thus rested solely upon its belief that the federal securities laws have "created a system providing equal access to information necessary for reasoned and intelligent investment decisions." 588 F.2d, at 1362. The use by anyone of material information not generally available is fraudulent, this theory suggests, because such information gives certain buyers or sellers an unfair advantage over less informed buyers and sellers.

This reasoning suffers from two defects. First not every instance of financial unfairness constitutes fraudulent activity under § 10(b). See Santa Fe Industries Inc. v. Green, 430 U.S. 462, 474–477, 97 S.Ct. 1292, 1301– 1303, 51 L.Ed.2d 480 (1977). Second, the element required to make silence fraudulent—a duty to disclose—is absent in this case. No duty could arise from petitioner's relationship with the sellers of the target company's securities, for petitioner had no prior dealings with them. He was not their agent, he was not a fiduciary, he was not a person in whom the sellers had placed their trust and confidence. He was, in fact, a complete stranger who dealt with the sellers only through impersonal market transactions.

We cannot affirm petitioner's conviction without recognizing a general duty between all participants in market transactions to forgo actions based on material, nonpublic information. Formulation of such a broad duty, which departs radically from the established doctrine that duty arises from a specific relationship between two parties, . . . should not be undertaken absent some explicit evidence of congressional intent.

As we have seen, no such evidence emerges from the language or legislative history of § 10(b). Moreover, neither the Congress nor the Commission ever has adopted a parity-of-information rule. Instead the problems caused by misuse of market information have been addressed by detailed and sophisticated regulation that recognizes when use of market information may not harm operation of the securities markets. For example, the Williams Act limits but does not completely prohibit a tender offeror's purchases of target corporation stock before public announcement of the offer. Congress' careful action in this and other areas contrasts, and is in some tension, with the broad rule of liability we are asked to adopt in this case.

Indeed, the theory upon which the petitioner was convicted is at odds with the Commission's view of § 10(b) as applied to activity that has the same effect on sellers as the petitioner's purchasers. "Warehousing" takes place when a corporation gives advance notice of its intention to launch a tender offer to institutional investors who then are able to purchase stock in the target company before the tender offer is made public and the price of shares rises. In this case, as in warehousing, a buyer of securities purchases stock in a target corporation on the basis of market information which is unknown to the seller. In both of these situations, the seller's behavior presumably would be altered if he had the nonpublic information. Significantly, however, the Commission has acted to bar warehousing under its authority to regulate tender offers after recognizing that action under § 10(b) would rest on a "somewhat different theory" than that previously used to regulate insider trading as fraudulent activity.

We see no basis for applying such a new and different theory of liability in this case. As we have emphasized before, the 1934 Act cannot be read " 'more broadly than its language and the statutory scheme reasonably permit.' " Touche Ross & Co. v. Redington, 442 U.S. 560, 578, 99 S.Ct. 2479, 2490, 61 L.Ed.2d 82 (June 18, 1979), quoting SEC v. Sloan, 436 U.S. 103, 116, 98 S.Ct. 1702, 1711, 56 L.Ed.2d 148 (1978). Section 10(b) is aptly described as a catch-all provision, but what it catches must be fraud. When an allegation of fraud is based upon nondisclosure, there can be no fraud absent a duty to speak. We hold that a duty to disclose under § 10(b) does not arise from the mere possession of nonpublic market information. The contrary result is without support in the legislative history of § 10(b) and would be inconsistent with the careful plan that Congress has enacted for regulation of the securities markets. Cf. Santa Fe Industries Inc. v. Green, 430 U.S., at 479, 97 S.Ct., at 1304.

IV

In its brief to this Court, the United States offers an alternative theory to support petitioner's conviction. It argues that petitioner breached a duty to the acquiring corporation when he acted upon information that he obtained by virtue of his position as an employee of a printer employed by the corporation. The breach of this duty is said to support a conviction under § 10(b) for fraud perpetrated upon both the acquiring corporation and the sellers.

We need not decide whether this theory has merit for it was not submitted to the jury. The jury was told, in the language of Rule 10b–5, that it could convict the petitioner if it concluded that he either (i) employed a device, scheme or artifice to defraud or (ii) engaged in an act, practice, or course of business which operated or would operate as a fraud or deceit upon any person. Record, at 681. The trial judge stated that a "scheme to defraud" is a plan to obtain money by trick or deceit and that "a failure by Chiarella to disclose material, non-public information in connection with his purchase of stock would constitute deceit." Id., at 683. Accordingly, the jury was instructed that the petitioner employed a scheme to defraud if he "did not disclose . . . material non-public information in connection with the purchases of the stock." Id., at 685–686.

Alternatively, the jury was instructed that it could convict if "Chiarella's alleged conduct of having purchased securities without disclosing material, nonpublic information would have or did have the effect of operating as a fraud upon a seller." Id., at 686. The judge earlier had stated that fraud "embraces all the means which human ingenuity can devise and which are resorted to by one individual to gain an advantage over another by false misrepresentation, suggestions or by suppression of the truth." Id., at 683.

The jury instructions demonstrate that petitioner was convicted merely because of his failure to disclose material, nonpublic information to sellers from whom he bought the stock of target corporations. The jury was not instructed on the nature or elements of a duty owed by petitioner to anyone other than the sellers. Because we cannot affirm a criminal conviction on the basis of a theory not presented to the jury, . . . we will not speculate upon whether such a duty exists, whether it has been breached, or whether such a breach constitutes a violation of § 10(b).

The judgment of the Court of Appeals is

Reversed.

[The following opinions are omitted: a concurring opinion by JUSTICE STEVENS, a concurring opinion by JUSTICE BRENNAN, a dissent by CHIEF JUSTICE BURGER and a dissent by JUSTICE BLACKMUN, joined in by JUSTICE MARSHALL].

HERMAN & MacLEAN v. HUDDLESTON

Supreme Court of the United States, 1983.

—— U.S. ——, 103 S.Ct. 683, —— L.Ed.2d ——.

[In 1969 Texas International Speedway, Inc. (TIS) raised $4,398,900 through a public securities offering based on a registration statement filed with the Securities and Exchange Commission. However, TIS went bankrupt in 1970 and 1972 Huddleston and Bradly filed a class action under Section 10(b) of the Securities Exchange Act of 1934 and Rule 10b–5. They joined as defendants most participants in the offering including the accountants, Herman & MacLean, who had given an opinion concerning the financial statements. A jury found for the plaintiffs after a three week trial. On appeal from the district court's judgment, the Court of Appeals reversed. The Supreme Court granted certiorari and, in an opinion by JUSTICE MARSHALL, (a) affirmed the Court of Appeals as to the right to maintain an action under Section 10(b) under the circumstances but (b) reversed its ruling that plaintiffs must prove this case by "clear and convincing evidence" rather than a "preponderance of the evidence." The excerpts that follow relate to point (a).]

II

The Securities Act of 1933 and the Securities Exchange Act of 1934 "constitute interrelated components of the federal regulatory scheme governing transactions in securities." Ernst & Ernst v. Hochfelder, 425 U.S. 185, 206, 96 S.Ct. 1375, 1387, 47 L.Ed.2d 668 (1976). The Acts created several express private rights of action, one of which is contained in Section 11 of the 1933 Act. In addition to the private actions created explicitly by the 1933 and 1934 Acts, federal courts have implied private remedies under other provisions of the two laws. Most significantly for present purposes, a private right of action under Section 10(b) of the 1934 Act and Rule 10b–5 has been consistently recognized for more than 35 years.[10] The existence of this implied remedy is simply beyond peradventure.

The issue in this case is whether a party should be barred from invoking this established remedy for fraud because the allegedly fraudulent conduct would apparently also provide the basis for a damage action under Section 11 of the 1933 Act. The resolution of this issue turns on the fact that the

---

10. The right of action was first recognized in Kardon v. National Gypsum Co., 69 F.Supp. 512 (ED Pa.1946). By 1961, four courts of appeals and several districts courts in other circuits had recognized the existence of a private remedy under Section 10(b) and Rule 10b–5, and only one district court decision had reached a contrary conclusion. See III L. Loss, Securities Regulation 1763–1764 and nn. 260–263 (2d ed. 1961) (collecting cases). By 1969, the existence of a private cause of action had been recognized by ten of the eleven courts of appeals. See VI L. Loss, Securities Regulation 3871–3873 (2d ed. Supp.1969) (collecting cases).

When the question whether an implied cause of action can be brought under Section 10(b) and Rule 10b–5 was first considered in this Court, we confirmed the existence of such a cause of action without extended discussion. See Superintendent of Insurance v. Bankers Life & Cas. Co., 404 U.S. 6, 13, n. 9, 92 S.Ct. 165, 169, n. 9, 30 L.Ed.2d 128 (1971). We have since repeatedly reaffirmed that "the existence of a private cause of action for violations of the statute and the Rule is now well established." Ernst & Ernst v. Hochfelder, supra, 425 U.S., at 196, 96 S.Ct., at 1382 (citing prior cases).

two provisions involve distinct causes of action and were intended to address different types of wrongdoing.

Section 11 of the 1933 Act allows purchasers of a registered security to sue certain enumerated parties in a registered offering when false or misleading information is included in a registration statement. The section was designed to assure compliance with the disclosure provisions of the Act by imposing a stringent standard of liability on the parties who play a direct role in a registered offering. If a plaintiff purchased a security issued pursuant to a registration statement, he need only show a material misstatement or omission to establish his *prima facie* case. Liability against the issuer of a security is virtually absolute, even for innocent misstatements. Other defendants bear the burden of demonstrating due diligence. See 15 U.S.C. § 77k(b).

Although limited in scope, Section 11 places a relatively minimal burden on a plaintiff. In contrast, Section 10(b) is a "catchall" antifraud provision, but it requires a plaintiff to carry a heavier burden to establish a cause of action. While a Section 11 action must be brought by a purchaser of a registered security, must be based on misstatements or omissions in a registration statement, and can only be brought against certain parties, a Section 10(b) action can be brought by a purchaser or seller of "*any* security" against "*any* person" who has used "*any* manipulative or deceptive device or contrivance" in connection with the purchase or sale of a security. 15 U.S.C. § 78j (emphasis added). However, a Section 10(b) plaintiff carries a heavier burden than a Section 11 plaintiff. Most significantly, he must prove that the defendant acted with scienter, i.e., with intent to deceive, manipulate, or defraud.

Since Section 11 and Section 10(b) address different types of wrongdoing, we see no reason to carve out an exception to Section 10(b) for fraud occurring in a registration statement just because the same conduct may also be actionable under Section 11. Exempting such conduct from liability under Section 10(b) would conflict with the basic purpose of the 1933 Act: to provide greater protection to purchasers of registered securities. It would be anomalous indeed if the special protection afforded to purchasers in a registered offering by the 1933 Act were deemed to deprive such purchasers of the protections against manipulation and deception that Section 10(b) makes available to all persons who deal in securities.

While some conduct actionable under Section 11 may also be actionable under Section 10(b), it is hardly a novel proposition that the Securities Exchange Act and the Securities Act "prohibit some of the same conduct." United States v. Naftalin, 441 U.S. 768, 778, 99 S.Ct. 2077, 2084, 60 L.Ed. 2d 624 (1979) . . . In savings clauses included in the 1933 and 1934 Acts, Congress rejected the notion that the express remedies of the securities laws would preempt all other rights of action. Section 16 of the 1933 Act states unequivocally that "[t]he rights and remedies provided by this subchapter shall be in addition to any and all other rights and remedies that may exist at law or in equity." 15 U.S.C. § 77p. Section 28(a) of the 1934 Act contains a parallel provision. 15 U.S.C. § 78bb(a). These provisions confirm that the remedies in each Act were to be supplemented by "any and all" additional remedies.

This conclusion is reinforced by our reasoning in Ernst & Ernst v. Hochfelder, supra, which held that actions under Section 10(b) require proof of scienter and do not encompass negligent conduct. In so holding, we noted that each of the express civil remedies in the 1933 Act allowing recovery for negligent conduct is subject to procedural restrictions not applicable to a Section 10(b) action.[18] 425 U.S., at 208–210, 96 S.Ct., at 1388–89. We emphasized that extension of Section 10(b) to negligent conduct would have allowed causes of action for negligence under the express remedies to be brought instead under Section 10(b), "thereby nullify[ing] the effectiveness of the carefully drawn procedural restrictions on these express actions." Id., at 210, 96 S.Ct., at 1389 (footnote omitted). In reasoning that scienter should be required in Section 10(b) actions in order to avoid circumvention of the procedural restrictions surrounding the express remedies, we necessarily assumed that the express remedies were not exclusive. Otherwise there would have been no danger of nullification. Conversely, because the added burden of proving scienter attaches to suits under Section 10(b), invocation of the Section 10(b) remedy will not "nullify" the procedural restrictions that apply to the express remedies.

This cumulative construction of the remedies under the 1933 and 1934 Acts is also supported by the fact that, when Congress comprehensively revised the securities laws in 1975, a consistent line of judicial decisions had permitted plaintiffs to sue under Section 10(b) regardless of the availability of express remedies. In 1975 Congress enacted the "most substantial and significant revision of this country's Federal securities laws since the passage of the Securities Exchange Act in 1934."[20] See Securities Acts Amendments of 1975, Pub.L. No. 94–29, 89 Stat. 97. When Congress acted, federal courts had consistently and routinely permitted a plaintiff to proceed under Section 10(b) even where express remedies under Section 11 or other provisions were available. In light of this well-established judicial interpretation, Congress' decision to leave Section 10(b) intact suggests that Congress ratified the cumulative nature of the Section 10(b) action. . . .

A cumulative construction of the securities laws also furthers their broad remedial purposes. In enacting the 1934 Act, Congress stated that its purpose was "to impose requirements necessary to make [securities] regulation and control reasonably complete and effective." 15 U.S.C. § 78b. In furtherance of that objective, Section 10(b) makes it unlawful to use "*any* manipulative or deceptive device or contrivance" in connection with the purchase or sale of any security. The effectiveness of the broad proscription against fraud in Section 10(b) would be undermined if its scope were restricted by the existence of an express remedy under Section 11. Yet we have

---

18. For example, a plaintiff in a Section 11 action may be required to post a bond for costs, 15 U.S.C. § 77k(e), and the statute of limitations is only one year, § 77m. In contrast, Section 10 (b) contains no provision requiring plaintiffs to post security for costs. Also, courts look to the most analogous statute of limitations of the forum state, which is usually longer than the

period provided for Section 11 actions. See Ernst & Ernst v. Hochfelder, supra, 425 U.S., at 210, n. 29, 96 S.Ct., at 1389, n. 29.

20. Securities Acts Amendments of 1975: Hearings on S. 249 Before the Subcomm. on Securities of the Senate Comm. on Banking, Housing and Urban Affairs, 94th Cong., 1st Sess. 1 (1975). . . .

repeatedly recognized that securities laws combating fraud should be construed "not technically and restrictively, but flexibly to effectuate [their] remedial purposes." SEC v. Capital Gains Research Bureau, 375 U.S. 180, 195, 84 S.Ct. 275, 284, 11 L.Ed.2d 237 (1963). . . . We therefore reject an interpretation of the securities laws that displaces an action under Section 10(b).

Accordingly, we hold that the availability of an express remedy under Section 11 of the 1933 Act does not preclude defrauded purchasers of registered securities from maintaining an action under Section 10(b) of the 1934 Act. To this extent the judgment of the court of appeals is affirmed.

EDGAR v. MITE CORP.

Supreme Court of the United States, 1982.
— U.S. —, 102 S.Ct. 2629, 73 L.Ed.2d 269.

[On January 19, 1979 MITE, a Delaware corporation with headquarters in Connecticut, initiated a cash tender offer for all outstanding shares (at $28 per share) of Chicago Rivet and Machine Co., a publicly held Illinois corporation. It filed a Schedule 14D–1 with the SEC in compliance with the Williams Act (§§ 13(d), 13(e) and 14(d)–(f) of the Securities Exchange Act). However, instead of complying with the Illinois Act, it filed an action in the United States District Court for the Northern District of Illinois to enjoin enforcement of that Act as preempted by federal law. Chicago Rivet unsuccessfully tried to stop MITE's offer by resort to the Pennsylvania Takeover Disclosure Law and then to the Illinois Act. The federal District Court issued first a preliminary and then a final, injunction against enforcement of the Illinois Act. Shortly thereafter MITE and Chicago Rivet entered into an agreement to withdraw the tender offer MITE had made and also one by Chicago Rivet seeking 40 percent of its own shares (at $30 per share); under the settlement MITE could examine the Chicago Rivet books and decide whether to renew a tender at $31 per share—which it decided not to do. Thereafter the Court of Appeals affirmed the District Court judgment and the Supreme Court first noted probable jurisdiction and then affirmed in an opinion by JUSTICE WHITE. The opinion commences by stating that the case was not moot since the Illinois Secretary of State indicated he intended to enforce the Act and impose civil and criminal penalties on MITE. Opinions by JUSTICES STEVENS, MARSHALL and REHNQUIST addressing the mootness question are omitted.]

We first address the holding that the Illinois Takeover Act is unconstitutional under the Supremacy Clause. We note at the outset that in passing the Williams Act, which is an amendment to the Securities and Exchange Act of 1934, Congress did not also amend § 28(a) of the 1934 Act, 15 U.S.C. § 78bb(a).[6] . . . Thus Congress did not explicitly prohibit states from

---

6. There is no evidence in the legislative history that Congress was aware of state takeover laws when it enacted the Williams Act. When the Williams Act was enacted in 1968, only Virginia had a takeover statute. The Virginia statute, Va.Code § 131–528, became effective March 5, 1968; the Williams Act was enacted several months later on July 19, 1968. Takeover statutes are now in effect in 37 states. Sargent, On the Validity of State Takeover Regulation: State Responses to *MITE* and *Kidwell*, 42 Ohio St.L.J. 689, 690 n. 7 (1981).

regulating takeovers; it left the determination whether the Illinois statute conflicts with the Williams Act to the courts. Of course, a state statute is void to the extent that it actually conflicts with a valid federal statute; and,

"[a] conflict will be found 'where compliance with both federal and state regulations is a physical impossibility . . .,' Florida Lime & Avocado Growers, Inc. v. Paul, 373 U.S. 132, 142–143 [83 S.Ct. 1210, 1217, 10 L.Ed.2d 248] (1963), or where the state 'law stands as an obstacle to the accomplishment and execution of the full purposes and objectives of Congress.' Hines v. Davidowitz, 312 U.S. 52, 67 [61 S.Ct. 399, 404, 85 L.Ed. 581] (1941); Jones v. Rath Packing Co., supra [430 U.S. 519] at 526, 540–541 [97 S.Ct. 1305, 1910, 1317, 51 L.Ed.2d 604]. Accord, De Canas v. Bica, 424 U.S. 351, 363 [96 S.Ct. 933, 940, 47 L.Ed.2d 43] (1976)." Ray v. Atlantic Richfield Co., 435 U.S. 151, 158 [98 S.Ct. 988, 994, 55 L.Ed.2d 179] (1978).

Our inquiry is not further narrowed in this case since there is no contention that it would be impossible to comply with both the provisions of the Williams Act and the more burdensome requirements of the Illinois law. The issue thus is, at it was in the Court of Appeals, whether the Illinois Act frustrates the objectives of the Williams Act in some substantial way.

The Williams Act, passed in 1968, was the congressional response to the increased use of cash tender offers in corporate acquisitions, a device that had "removed a substantial number of corporate control contests from the reach of existing disclosure requirements of the federal securities laws." Piper v. Chris-Craft Industries, 430 U.S. 1, 22 [97 S.Ct. 926, 939, 51 L.Ed. 2d 124] (1977). The Williams Act filed this regulatory gap. [A summary of the Act's provisions is omitted].

There is no question that in imposing these requirements, Congress intended to protect investors. Piper v. Chris-Craft Industries, supra, at 35, 97 S.Ct. at 946; Rondeau v. Mosinee Paper Corp., 422 U.S. 49, 58, 95 S.Ct. 2069, 2075, 45 L.Ed.2d 12 (1975); S.Rep.No.550, 90th Cong., 1st Sess. 3–4 (1967) ("Senate Report"). But it is also crystal clear that a major aspect of the effort to protect the investor was to avoid favoring either management or the takeover bidder. As we noted in *Piper*, the disclosure provisions originally embodied in S. 2731 "were avowedly pro-management in the target company's efforts to defeat takeover bids." 430 U.S., at 30, 97 S.Ct., at 943. But Congress became convinced "that takeover bids should not be discouraged because they serve a useful purpose in providing a check on entrenched but inefficient management." Senate Report at 3.[9] It also became apparent that entrenched management was often successful in defeating takeover attempts. As the legislation evolved, therefore, Congress disclaimed any "intention to provide a weapon for management to discourage takeover bids . . ." Rondeau v. Mosinee Paper Corp., supra, 422 U.S., at 58, 95 S.Ct., at 2075, and expressly embraced a policy of neutrality. As Senator Williams explained, "We have taken extreme care to avoid tipping the scales

---

9. Congress also did not want to deny shareholders "the opportunities which result from the competitive bidding for a block of stock of a given company," namely the opportunity to sell shares for a premium over their market price. 113 Cong.Rec. 24666 (1967) (remarks of Sen. Javits).

either in favor of management or in favor of the persons making the take-over bids." 113 Cong.Rec. 24664 (1967). This policy of "evenhandedness," Piper v. Chris-Craft Industries, supra, 430 U.S., at 31, 97 S.Ct., at 944, represented a conviction that neither side in the contest should be extended additional advantages vis-a-vis the investor, who if furnished with adequate information would be in a position to make his own informed choice. We, therefore, agree with the Court of Appeals that Congress sought to protect the investor not only by furnishing him with the necessary information but also by withholding from management or the bidder any undue advantage that could frustrate the exercise of an informed choice. 633 F.2d, at 496.

To implement this policy of investor protection while maintaining the balance between management and the bidder, Congress required the latter to file with the Commission and furnish the company and the investor with all information adequate to the occasion. With that filing, the offer could go forward, stock could be tendered and purchased, but a stockholder was free within a specified time to withdraw his tendered shares. He was also protected if the offer was increased. Looking at this history as a whole, it appears to us, as it did to the Court of Appeals, that Congress intended to strike a balance between the investor, management and the takeover bidder. The bidder was to furnish the investor and the target company with adequate information but there was no "intention to do . . . more than give incumbent management an opportunity to express and explain its position." Rondeau v. Mosinee Paper Corp., supra, 422 U.S., at 58, 95 S.Ct., at 2075. Once that opportunity was extended, Congress anticipated that the investor, if he so chose, and the takeover bidder should be free to move forward within the time-frame provided by Congress.

IV

The Court of Appeals identified three provisions of the Illinois Act that upset the careful balance struck by Congress and which therefore stand as obstacles to the accomplishment and execution of the full purposes and objectives of Congress. We agree with the Court of Appeals in all essential respects.

A

The Illinois Act requires a tender offeror to notify the Secretary of State and the target company of its intent to make a tender offer and the material terms of the offer 20 business days before the offer becomes effective. Ill. Rev.Stat., ch. 121½, ¶¶ 137.54.E, 137.54.B (1979). During that time, the offeror may not communicate its offer to the shareholders. Id., at ¶ 137.54.A. Meanwhile, the target company is free to disseminate information to its shareholders concerning the impending offer. The contrast with the Williams Act is apparent. Under that Act, there is no pre-commencement notification requirement; the critical date is the date a tender offer is "first published or sent or given to security holders." 15 U.S.C. § 78n(d)(1). See also 17 CFR § 240.14d–2 (1981).

We agree with the Court of Appeals that by providing the target company with additional time within which to take steps to combat the offer, the precommencement notification provisions furnish incumbent management with a powerful tool to combat tender offers, perhaps to the detriment of the stockholders who will not have an offer before them during this period. These consequences are precisely what Congress determined should be avoided, and for this reason, the precommencement notification provision frustrates the objectives of the Williams Act.

It is important to note in this respect that in the course of events leading to the adoption of the Williams Act, Congress several times refused to impose a pre-commencement disclosure requirement. . . . Congress rejected another pre-commencement notification proposal during deliberations of the 1970 amendments to the Williams Act.

B

For similar reasons, we agree with the Court of Appeals that the hearing provisions of the Illinois Act frustrate the congressional purpose by introducing extended delay into the tender offer process. The Illinois Act allows the Secretary of State to call a hearing with respect to any tender offer subject to the Act, and the offer may not proceed until the hearing is completed. Ill.Rev.Stat., ch. 121½, ¶¶ 137.57.A and B (1979). The Secretary may call a hearing at any time prior to the commencement of the offer, and there is no deadline for the completion of the hearing. Id., at ¶¶ 137.57.C and D. Although the Secretary is to render a decision within 15 days after the conclusion of the hearing, that period may be extended without limitation. Not only does the Secretary of State have the power to delay a tender offer indefinitely, but incumbent management may also use the hearing provisions of the Illinois Act to delay a tender offer. The Secretary is required to call a hearing if requested to do so by, among other persons, those who are located in Illinois "as determined by post office address as shown on the records of the target company and who hold of record or beneficially, or both, at least 10% of the outstanding shares of any class of equity securities which is the subject of the takeover offer." Id., at ¶ 137.57.A. Since incumbent management in many cases will control, either directly or indirectly, 10% of the target company's shares, this provision allows management to delay the commencement of an offer by insisting on a hearing. As the Court of Appeals observed, these provisions potentially afford management a "powerful weapon to stymie indefinitely a takeover." 633 F.2d, at 494.[12] In enacting the Williams Act, Congress itself "recognized that delay can seriously impede a tender offer" and sought to avoid it. Great Western United Corp. v. Kidwell, 577 F.2d 1256, 1277 (CA5 1978); Senate Report at 4.[13]

---

12. Delay has been characterized as "the most potent weapon in a tender offer fight." Langevoort, State Tender-Offer Legislation: Interests, Effects, and Political Competency, 62 Cornell L.Rev. 213, 238 (1977). See also Wachtell, Special Tender Offer Litigation Tactics, 32 Bus.L. 1433, 1437–1442 (1977); Wilner and Landy, The Tender Trap. State Takeover Laws and Their Constitutionality, 45 Ford. L.Rev. 1, 9–10 (1976).

13. According to the Securities and Exchange Commission, delay enables a target company to:

"(1) repurchase its own securities;

"(2) announce dividend increases or stock splits;

"(3) issue additional shares of stock;

"(4) acquire other companies to produce an antitrust violation should the tender offer succeed;

"(5) arrange a defensive merger;

Congress reemphasized the consequences of delay when it enacted the Hart-Scott-Rodino Antitrust Improvements Act, Pub.L. No. 94–435, 90 Stat. 1383, 15 U.S.C. § 12 et seq.

> "[I]t is clear that this short waiting period [the ten-day period for proration provided for by § 14(d)(6) of the Securities Exchange Act, which applies only after a tender offer is commenced] was founded on congressional concern that a longer delay might unduly favor the target firm's incumbent management, and permit them to frustrate many pro-competitive cash tenders. This ten-day waiting period thus underscores the basic purpose of the Williams Act —to maintain a neutral policy towards cash tender offers, by avoiding lengthy delays that might discourage their chances for success."
> H.R.Rep.No.94–1373, 94th Cong., 2d Sess. 12 (1976),[14] U.S.Code Cong. & Admin.News, pp. 2572, 2644.

As we have said, Congress anticipated investors and the takeover offeror be free to go forward without unreasonable delay. The potential for delay provided by the hearing provisions upset the balance struck by Congress by favoring management at the expense of stockholders. We therefore agree with the Court of Appeals that these hearing provisions conflict with the Williams Act.

C

The Court of Appeals also concluded that the Illinois Act is pre-empted by the Williams Act insofar as it allows the Secretary of State of Illinois to pass on the substantive fairness of a tender offer. Under ¶ 137.57.E of the Illinois law, the Secretary is required to deny registration of a takeover offer if he finds that the offer "fails to provide full and fair disclosure to the offerees . . . *or that the take-over offer is inequitable . . . .*" (Emphasis added) The Court of Appeals understood the Williams Act and its legislative history to indicate that Congress intended for investors to

---

"(6) enter into restrictive loan agreements,

"(7) institute litigation challenging the tender offer." Brief for the Securities and Exchange Commission as *amicus curiae* 10, n. 8.

14. Representative Rodino set out the consequences of delay in greater detail when he described the relationship between the Hart-Scott-Rodino Act and the Williams Act:

"In the case of cash tender offers, more so than in other mergers, the equities include time and the danger of undue delay. This bill is no way intends to repeal or reverse the congressional purpose underlying the 1968 Williams Act, or the 1970 amendments to that act. . . . Lengthier delays will give the target firm plenty of time to defeat the offer, by abolishing cumulative voting, arranging a speedy defense merger,

quickly incorporating in a State with an anti-takeover statute, or negotiating costly lifetime employment contracts for incumbent management. And the longer the waiting period, the more the target's stock may be bid up in the market, making the offer more costly—and less successful. Should this happen, it will mean that shareholders of the target firm will be effectively deprived of the choice that cash tenders give to them: Either accept the offer and thereby gain the tendered premium, or reject the offer. Generally, the courts have construed the Williams Act so as to maintain these two options for the target company's shareholders, and the House Conferees contemplate that the courts will continue to do so." 122 Cong.Rec. 30877 (1976).

be free to make their own decisions. We agree. Both the House and Senate Reports observed that the Act was "designed to make the relevant facts known so that shareholders have a fair opportunity to make their decision." H.R.Rep.No.1711, 90th Cong., 2d Sess. 3 (1968), U.S.Code Cong. & Admin. News, pp. 2811, 2813; Senate Report at 3. Thus, as the Court of Appeals said, "[t]he state thus offers investor protection at the expense of investor autonomy—an approach quite in conflict with that adopted by Congress." 633 F.2d at 494.

V

The Commerce Clause provides that "Congress shall have Power .   .   . [t]o regulate Commerce   .   .   .   among the several states." U.S.Const., Art. 1, § 8, cl. 3. "[A]t least since Cooley v. Board of Wardens, 53 U.S. (12 How.) 299, 13 L.Ed. 996 (1852) it has been clear that 'the Commerce Clause. .   .   .   even without implementing legislation by Congress is a limitation upon the power of the States.'" Great Atlantic & Pacific Tea Co. v. Cottrell, 424 U.S. 366, 370–371, 96 S.Ct. 923, 927, 47 L.Ed.2d 55 (1976), quoting Freeman v. Hewitt, 329 U.S. 249, 252, 67 S.Ct. 274, 276, 91 L.Ed. 265 (1946). See also Lewis v. BT Investment Managers, Inc., 447 U.S. 27, 35, 100 S.Ct. 2009, 2014, 64 L.Ed.2d 702 (1980). Not every exercise of state power with some impact on interstate commerce is invalid. A state statute must be upheld if it "regulates even-handedly to effectuate a legitimate local public interest, and its effects on interstate commerce are only incidental   .   .   . unless the burden imposed on such commerce is clearly excessive in relation to the putative local benefits." Pike v. Bruce Church, Inc., 397 U.S. 137, 142, 90 S.Ct. 844, 847, 25 L.Ed.2d 174 (1970), citing Huron Cement Co. v. Detroit, 362 U.S. 440, 443, 80 S.Ct. 813, 815, 4 L.Ed.2d 852 (1960). The Commerce Clause, however, permits only *incidental* regulation of interstate commerce by the states; direct regulation is prohibited. Shafer v. Farmers Grain Co., 268 U.S. 189, 199, 45 S.Ct. 481, 485, 69 L.Ed. 909 (1925). See also Pike v. Bruce Church, Inc., supra, 397 U.S., at 142, 90 S.Ct., at 847. The Illinois Act violates these principles for two reasons. First, it directly regulates and prevents, unless its terms are satisfied, interstate tender offers which in turn would generate interstate transactions. Second, the burden the Act imposes on interstate commerce is excessive in light of the local interests the Act purports to further.

A

States have traditionally regulated intrastate securities transactions, and this Court has upheld the authority of states to enact "blue-sky" laws against Commerce Clause, challenges on several occasions. Hall v. Geiger-Jones Co., 242 U.S. 539, 37 S.Ct. 217, 61 L.Ed. 480 (1917); Caldwell v. Sioux Falls Stock Yards Co., 242 U.S. 559, 37 S.Ct. 224, 61 L.Ed. 493 (1917); Merrick v. N. W. Halsey & Co., 242 U.S. 568, 37 S.Ct. 227, 61 L.Ed. 498 (1917). The Court's rationale for upholding blue-sky laws was that they only regulated transactions occurring within the regulating states. "The provisions of the law   .   .   .   apply to dispositions of securities *within* the State and while information of those issued in other States and foreign countries is required to be filed   .   .   .   they are only affected by the requirement of a license of one who deals with them *within* the State.   .   .   .   Such regulations affect interstate commerce in securities only incidentally." Hall v. Geiger-Jones Co., supra, 242 U.S., at 557–558, 37 S.Ct., at 223 (cites omitted). Congress has also recognized the validity of such laws governing intrastate securities transactions in § 28(a) of the Securities Exchange Act, 15 U.S.C. § 78bb(a), a provision "designed to save state blue-sky laws from preemption." Leroy v. Great Western United Corp., 443 U.S. 173, 182, n. 13, 99 S.Ct. 2710, 2716, n. 13, 61 L.Ed.2d 464 (1979).

The Illinois Act differs substantially from state blue-sky laws in that it directly regulates transactions which take place across state lines, even if wholly outside the State of Illinois. A tender offer for securities of a publicly-held corporation is ordinarily communicated by the use of the mails or other means of interstate commerce to shareholders across the country and abroad. Securities are tendered and transactions closed by similar means. Thus, in this case, MITE Corporation, the tender offeror, is a Delaware corporation with principal offices in Connecticut. Chicago Rivet is a publicly-held Illinois corporation with shareholders scattered around the country, 27% of whom live in Illinois. MITE's offer to Chicago Rivet's shareholders, including those in Illinois, necessarily employed interstate facilities in communicating its offer, which, if accepted, would result in transactions occurring across state lines. These transactions would themselves be interstate commerce. Yet the Illinois law, unless complied with, sought to prevent MITE from making its offer and concluding interstate transactions not only with Chicago Rivet's stockholders living in Illinois, but also with those living in other states and having no connection with Illinois. Indeed, the Illinois law on its face would apply even if not a single one of Chicago Rivet's shareholders were a resident of Illinois, since the Act applies to every tender offer for a corporation meeting two of the following conditions: the corporation has its principal executive office in Illinois, is organized under Illinois laws, or has at least 10% of its stated capital and paid-in surplus represented in Illinois. Ill.Rev.Stat., ch. 121½, ¶ 137.52–10.(2) (1979). Thus the Act could be applied to regulate a tender offer which would not affect a single Illinois shareholder.

It is therefore apparent that the Illinois statute is a direct restraint on interstate commerce and that it has a sweeping extraterritorial effect. Furthermore, if Illinois may impose such regulations, so may other states; and interstate commerce in securities transactions generated by tender offers would be thoroughly stifled. . . . The Commerce Clause also precludes the application of a state statute to commerce that takes place wholly outside of the state's borders, whether or not the commerce has effects within the state. . . . Because the Illinois Act purports to regulate directly and to interdict interstate commerce, including commerce wholly outside the state, it must be held invalid as were the laws at issue in *Shaffer* and *Southern Pacific.*

B

The Illinois Act is also unconstitutional under the test of Pike v. Bruce Church, Inc., 397 U.S., at 142, 90 S.Ct., at 847, for even when a state statute regulates interstate commerce indirectly, the burden imposed on that commerce must not be excessive in relation to the local interests served by the statute. The most obvious burden the Illinois Act imposes on interstate commerce arises from the statute's previously-described nationwide reach which purports to give Illinois the power to determine whether a tender offer may proceed anywhere.

The effects of allowing the Illinois Secretary of State to block a nationwide tender offer are substantial. Shareholders are deprived of the opportunity to sell their shares at a premium. The reallocation of economic resources to their highest-valued use, a process which can improve efficiency and competition, is hindered. The incentive the tender offer mechanism provides incumbent management to perform well so that stock prices remain high is reduced. See Easterbrook and Fischel, The Proper Role of a Target's Management in Responding to a Tender Offer, 94 Harv.L.Rev. 1161, 1173–1174 (1981); Fischel, Efficient Capital Market Theory, the Market for Corporate Control and the Regulation of Cash Tender Offers, 57 Tex.L.Rev. 1, 5, 27–28, 45 (1978); H.R.Rep.No.94–1373, 94th Cong., 2d Sess. 12 (1976).

Appellant claims the Illinois Act furthers two legitimate local interests. He argues that Illinois seeks to protect resident security holders and that the Act merely regulates the internal affairs of companies incorporated under Illinois law. We agree with the Court of Appeals that these asserted interests are insufficient to outweigh the burdens Illinois imposes on interstate commerce.

While protecting local investors is plainly a legitimate state objective, the state has no legitimate interest in protecting non-resident shareholders. Insofar as the Illinois law burdens out-of-state transactions, there is nothing to be weighed in the balance to sustain the law. We note, furthermore, that the Act completely exempts from coverage a corporation's acquisition of its own shares. Ill.Rev.Stat., ch. 121½, ¶ 137.52–9.(4). Thus Chicago Rivet was able to make a competing tender offer for its own stock without complying with the Illinois Act, leaving Chicago Rivet's shareholders to depend only on the protections afforded them by federal securities law, protections· which Illinois views as inadequate to protect investors in other contexts. This distinction is at variance with Illinois' asserted legislative purpose, and tends to undermine appellant's justification for the burdens the statute imposes on interstate commerce.

We are also unconvinced that the Illinois Act substantially enhances the shareholders' position. The Illinois Act seeks to protect shareholders of a company subject to a tender offer by requiring disclosures regarding the offer, assuring that shareholders have adequate time to decide whether to tender their shares, and according shareholders withdrawal, proration and equal consideration rights. However, the Williams Act provides these same substantive protections, compare Ill.Rev.Stat., ch. 121½, ¶¶ 137.59.C, D, and E (1979) (withdrawal, proration, and equal consideration rights) with 15 U.S.C. § 78n(d)(5), (6) and (7) and 17 CFR § 240.14d–7 (1981) (same). As the Court of Appeals noted, the disclosures required by the Illinois Act which go beyond those mandated by the Williams Act and the regulations pursuant to it may not substantially enhance the shareholders' ability to make informed decisions. 633 F.2d, at 500. It also was of the view that the possible benefits of the potential delays required by the Act may be outweighed by the increased risk that the tender offer will fail due to defensive tactics employed by incumbent management. We are unprepared to disagree with the Court of Appeals in these respects, and conclude that the protections the Illinois Act affords resident security holders are, for the most part, speculative.

Appellant also contends that Illinois has an interest in regulating the internal affairs of a corporation incorporated under its laws. The internal affairs doctrine is a conflict of laws principle which recognizes that only one state should have the authority to regulate a corporation's internal affairs—matters peculiar to the relationships among or between the corporation and its current officers, directors, and shareholders—because otherwise a corporation could be faced with conflicting demands. See Restatement (Second) of Conflict of Laws, § 302, Comment b at 307–308 (1971). That doctrine is of little use to the state in this context. Tender offers contemplate transfers of stock by stockholders to a third party and do not themselves implicate the internal affairs of the target company. Great Western United Corp. v. Kidwell, 577 F.2d, at 1280, n. 53; Restatement, supra, § 302, comment e at 310. Furthermore, the proposed justification is somewhat incredible since the Illinois Act applies to tender offers for any corporation for which 10% of the outstanding shares are held by Illinois residents, Ill. Rev.Stat., ch. 121½, ¶ 137.52–10 (1979). The Act thus applies to corporations that are not incorporated in Illinois and have their principal place of business in other states. Illinois has no interest in regulating the internal affairs of foreign corporations.

We conclude with the Court of Appeals that the Illinois Act imposes a substantial burden on interstate commerce which outweighs its putative local benefits. It is accordingly invalid under the Commerce Clause.

The judgment of the Court of Appeals is

Affirmed.

JUSTICE POWELL, concurring in part.

I agree with JUSTICE MARSHALL that this case is moot. In view, however, of the decision of a majority of the Court to reach the merits, I join Parts I and V–B of the Court's opinion.

I join Part V–B because its Commerce Clause reasoning leaves some room for state regulation of tender offers. This period in our history is marked by conglomerate corporate formations essentially unrestricted by the antitrust laws. Often the offeror possesses resources, in terms of professional personnel experienced in takeovers as well as of capital, that vastly exceed those of the takeover target. This disparity in resources may seriously disadvantage a relatively small or regional target corporation. Inevitably there are certain adverse consequences in terms of general public interest when corporate headquarters are moved away from a city and State.*

---

* The corporate headquarters of the great national and multinational corporations tend to be located in the large cities of a few States. When corporate headquarters are transferred out of a city and State into one of these metropolitan centers, the State and locality from which the transfer is made inevitably suffer significantly. Management personnel—many of whom have provided community leadership—may move to the new corporate headquarters. Contributions to cultural, charitable and educational life—both in terms of leadership and financial support—also tend to diminish when there is a move of corporate headquarters.

The Williams Act provisions, implementing a policy of neutrality, seem to assume corporate entities of substantially equal resources. I agree with Justice Stevens that the Williams Act's neutrality policy does not necessarily imply a congressional intent to prohibit state legislation designed to assure— at least in some circumstances—greater protection to interests that include but often are broader than those of incumbent management.

JUSTICE O'CONNOR, concurring in part.

I agree with the Court that the case is not moot, and that portions of the Illinois Business Take-Over Act, Ill.Rev.Stat., ch. 121½, ¶ 137.51 et seq. (1979), are invalid under the Commerce Clause. Because it is not necessary to reach the preemption issue, I join only Parts I, II and V of the Court's opinion, and would affirm the judgment of the Court of Appeals on that basis.

WEINBERGER v. UOP, INC.
Supreme Court of Delaware, 1983.
457 A.2d 701.

[The Signal Companies, Inc. (Signal) is a diversified, technically based corporation. Its stock is publicly traded on the New York and other stock exchanges. In 1974, after selling off a subsidiary, Signal looked for a use for its cash surplus. It hit upon UOP, also a diversified industrial corporation. UOP's stock was trading on the New York Stock Exchange at just under $14 per share. As a result of a cash tender offer and a purchase by Signal of 1,500,000 shares of UOP's authorized but unissued stock, Signal acquired in the spring of 1975 50.5 percent of the stock of UOP at $21 per share. Of UOP's board six were Signal's nominees. After searching for other investment candidates, Signal in 1978 decided to acquire the remaining 49.5 percent of UOP's stock. The study leading up to the acquisition was made by two Signal officers, Arledge and Chitiea, who were also directors of both Signal and UOP. Although they concluded that UOP shares were a good investment at up to $24, Signal ultimately proposed a merger at $21 per UOP share. At the UOP board meeting a Lehman Brothers opinion letter finding $21 to be a fair price was available but not the Arledge-Chitiea report. The merger was accepted by the UOP board with Signal's directors abstaining from voting. The merger was submitted to the May 1978 annual meeting of UOP's shareholders. 56 percent of the minority shares voted, 51.9 percent in favor of the merger and 4.1 percent against—with Signal's holdings a total of 76.2 percent for and 2.2 percent opposed. The merger became effective on May 26, 1978. Plaintiff, a former UOP shareholder, brought a class action challenging the merger. The Chancellor, finding the terms fair, entered judgment for defendants. On appeal and after rehearing en banc, the Supreme Court reversed and remanded in an opinion by JUSTICE MOORE:]

II.

A.

A primary issue mandating reversal is the preparation by two UOP directors, Arledge and Chitiea, of their feasibility study for the exclusive use and benefit of Signal. This document was of obvious significance to both

Signal and UOP. Using UOP data, it described the advantages to Signal of ousting the minority at a price range of $21–$24 per share. Mr. Arledge, one of the authors, outlined the benefits to Signal: [6]

Purpose Of The Merger

(1) Provides an outstanding investment opportunity for Signal—(Better than any recent acquisition we have seen.)

(2) Increases Signal's earnings.

(3) Facilitates the flow of resources between Signal and its subsidiaries —(Big factor—works both ways.)

(4) Provides cost savings potential for Signal and UOP.

(5) Improves the percentage of Signal's "operating earnings" as opposed to "holding company earnings".

(6) Simplifies the understanding of Signal.

(7) Facilitates technological exchange among Signal's subsidiaries.

(8) Eliminates potential conflicts of interest.

Having written those words, solely for the use of Signal, it is clear from the record that neither Arledge nor Chitiea shared this report with their fellow directors of UOP. We are satisfied that no one else did either. This conduct hardly meets the fiduciary standards applicable to such a transaction.

. . .

The Arledge-Chitiea report speaks for itself in supporting the Chancellor's finding that a price of up to $24 was a "good investment" for Signal. It shows that a return on the investment at $21 would be 15.7% versus 15.5% at $24 per share. This was a difference of only two-tenths of one percent, while it meant over $17,000,000 to the minority. Under such circumstances, paying UOP's minority shareholders $24 would have had relatively little long-term effect on Signal, and the Chancellor's findings concerning the benefit to Signal, even at a price of $24, were obviously correct. Levitt v. Bouvier, Del.Supr., 287 A.2d 671, 673 (1972).

Certainly, this was a matter of material significance to UOP and its shareholders. Since the study was prepared by two UOP directors, using UOP information for the exclusive benefit of Signal, and nothing whatever was done to disclose it to the outside UOP directors or the minority shareholders, a question of breach of fiduciary duty arises. This problem occurs because there were common Signal-UOP directors participating, at least to some extent, in the UOP board's decision-making processes without full disclosure of the conflicts they faced.[7]

---

6. The parentheses indicate certain handwritten comments of Mr. Arledge.

7. Although perfection is not possible, or expected, the result here could have been entirely different if UOP had appointed an independent negotiating committee of its outside directors to deal with Signal at arm's length. See, e.g., Harriman v. E. I. duPont de Nemours & Co., 411 F.Supp. 133 (D.Del.

1975). Since fairness in this context can be equated to conduct by a theoretical, wholly independent, board of directors acting upon the matter before them, it is unfortunate that this course apparently was neither considered nor pursued. Johnston v. Greene, Del.Supr., 121 A.2d 919, 925 (1956). Particularly in a parent-subsidiary context, a showing that the action taken was as though each of the contending parties

B.

In assessing this situation, the Court of Chancery was required to: examine what information defendants had and to measure it against what they gave to the minority stockholders, in a context in which "complete candor" is required. In other words, the limited function of the Court was to determine whether defendants had disclosed all information in their possession germane to the transaction in issue. And by "germane" we mean, for present purposes, information such as a reasonable shareholder would consider important in deciding whether to sell or retain stock.

. . .

. . . Completeness, not adequacy, is both the norm and the mandate under present circumstances.

Lynch v. Vickers Energy Corp., Del.Supr., 383 A.2d 278, 281 (1977) (*Lynch I*). This is merely stating in another way the long-existing principle of Delaware law that these Signal designated directors on UOP's board still owed UOP and its shareholders an uncompromising duty of loyalty.

. . .

Given the absence of any attempt to structure this transaction on an arm's length basis, Signal cannot escape the effects of the conflicts it faced, particularly when its designees on UOP's board did not totally abstain from participation in the matter. There is no "safe harbor" for such divided loyalties in Delaware. When directors of a Delaware corporation are on both sides of a transaction, they are required to demonstrate their utmost good faith and the most scrupulous inherent fairness of the bargain. Gottlieb v. Heyden Chemical Corp., Del.Supr., 91 A.2d 57, 57–58 (1952). The requirement of fairness is unflinching in its demand that where one stands on both sides of a transaction, he has the burden of establishing its entire fairness, sufficient to pass the test of careful scrutiny by the courts. . . .

There is no dilution of this obligation where one holds dual or multiple directorships, as in a parent-subsidiary context. Levien v. Sinclair Oil Corp., Del.Ch., 261 A.2d 911, 915 (1969.) Thus, individuals who act in a dual capacity as directors of two corporations, one of whom is parent and the other subsidiary, owe the same duty of good management to both corporations, and in the absence of an independent negotiating structure (see note 7, supra), or the directors' total abstention from any participation in the matter, this duty is to be exercised in light of what is best for both companies. Warshaw v. Calhoun, Del.Supr., 221 A.2d 487, 492 (1966). The record demonstrates that Signal has not met this obligation.

had in fact exerted its bargaining power against the other at arm's length is strong evidence that the transaction meets the test of fairness. Getty Oil Co. v. Skelly Oil Co., Del.Supr., 267 A. 2d 883, 886 (1970); Puma v. Marriott, Del.Ch., 283 A.2d 693, 696 (1971).

C.

The concept of fairness has two basic aspects: fair dealing and fair price. The former embraces questions of when the transaction was timed, how it was initiated, structured, negotiated, disclosed to the directors, and how the approvals of the directors and the stockholders were obtained.   The latter aspect of fairness relates to the economic and financial considerations of the proposed merger, including all relevant factors: assets, market value, earnings, future prospects, and any other elements that affect the intrinsic or inherent value of a company's stock.   Moore, The "Interested" Director or Officer Transaction, 4 Del.J.Corp.L. 674, 676 (1979); Nathan & Shapiro, Legal Standard of Fairness of Merger Terms Under Delaware Law, 2 Del.J.Corp.L. 44, 46–47 (1977). See Tri-Continental Corp. v. Battye, Del.Supr., 74 A.2d 71, 72 (1950); 8 Del.C. § 262(h).   However, the test for fairness is not a bifurcated one as between fair dealing and price. All aspects of the issue must be examined as a whole since the question is one of entire fairness.   However, in a non-fraudulent transaction we recognize that price may be the preponderant consideration outweighing other features of the merger.   Here, we address the two basic aspects of fairness separately because we find reversible error as to both.

D.

Part of fair dealing is the obvious duty of candor required by *Lynch I*, supra.   Moreover, one possessing superior knowledge may not mislead any stockholder by use of corporate information to which the latter is not privy. Lank v. Steiner, Del.Supr., 224 A.2d 242, 244 (1966).   Delaware has long imposed this duty even upon persons who are not corporate officers or directors, but who nonetheless are privy to matters of interest or significance to their company.   Brophy v. Cities Service Co., Del.Ch., 70 A.2d 5, 7 (1949). With the well-established Delaware law on the subject, and the Court of Chancery's findings of fact here, it is inevitable that the obvious conflicts posed by Arledge and Chitiea's preparation of their "feasibility study", derived from UOP information, for the sole use and benefit of Signal, cannot pass muster.

The Arledge-Chitiea report is but one aspect of the element of fair dealing.   How did this merger evolve?   It is clear that it was entirely initiated by Signal.   The serious time constraints under which the principals acted were all set by Signal.   It had not found a suitable outlet for its excess cash and considered UOP a desirable investment, particularly since it was now in a position to acquire the whole company for itself.   For whatever reasons, and they were only Signal's, the entire transaction was presented to and approved by UOP's board within four business days.   Standing alone, this is not necessarily indicative of any lack of fairness by a majority shareholder.   It was what occurred, or more properly, what did not occur, during this brief period that makes the time constraints imposed by Signal relevant to the issue of fairness.

The structure of the transaction, again, was Signal's doing.   So far as negotiations were concerned, it is clear that they were modest at best.   Crawford, Signal's man at UOP, never really talked price with Signal, except to accede to its management's statements on the subject, and to convey to Signal the UOP outside directors' view that as between the $20–$21 range under consideration, it would have to be $21. The latter is not a surprising outcome, but hardly arm's length negotiations. Only the protection of benefits for UOP's key employees and the issue of Lehman Brothers' fee approached any concept of bargaining.

As we have noted, the matter of disclosure to the UOP directors was wholly flawed by the conflicts of interest raised by the Arledge-Chitiea report. All of those conflicts were resolved by Signal in its own favor without divulging any aspect of them to UOP.

This cannot but undermine a conclusion that this merger meets any reasonable test of fairness. The outside UOP directors lacked one material piece of information generated by two of their colleagues, but shared only with Signal. True, the UOP board had the Lehman Brothers' fairness opinion, but that firm has been blamed by the plaintiff for the hurried task it performed, when more properly the responsibility for this lies with Signal. There was no disclosure of the circumstances surrounding the rather cursory preparation of the Lehman Brothers' fairness opinion. Instead, the impression was given UOP's minority that a careful study had been made, when in fact speed was the hallmark, and Mr. Glanville, Lehman's partner in charge of the matter, and also a UOP director, having spent the weekend in Vermont, brought a draft of the "fairness opinion letter" to the UOP directors' meeting on March 6, 1978 with the price left blank. We can only conclude from the record that the rush imposed on Lehman Brothers by Signal's timetable contributed to the difficulties under which this investment banking firm attempted to perform its responsibilities. Yet, none of this was disclosed to UOP's minority.

Finally, the minority stockholders were denied the critical information that Signal considered a price of $24 to be a good investment. Since this would have meant over $17,000,000 more to the minority, we cannot conclude that the shareholder vote was an informed one. Under the circumstances, an approval by a majority of the minority was meaningless. *Lynch I*, 383 A.2d at 279, 281; Cahall v. Lofland, Del.Ch., 114 A.2d 224 (1921).

Given these particulars and the Delaware law on the subject, the record does not establish that this transaction satisfies any reasonable concept of fair dealing, and the Chancellor's findings in that regard must be reversed.

E.

Turning to the matter of price, plaintiff also challenges its fairness. His evidence was that on the date the merger was approved the stock was worth at least $26 per share. In support, he offered the testimony of a chartered investment analyst who used two basic approaches to valuation: a comparative analysis of the premium paid over market in ten other tender offer-merger combinations, and a discounted cash flow analysis.

In this breach of fiduciary duty case, the Chancellor perceived that the approach to valuation was the same as that in an appraisal proceeding.

Consistent with precedent, he rejected plaintiff's method of proof and accepted defendants' evidence of value as being in accord with practice under prior case law. This means that the so-called "Delaware block" or weighted average method was employed wherein the elements of value, i.e., assets, market price, earnings, etc., were assigned a particular weight and the resulting amounts added to determine the value per share. This procedure has been in use for decades. See In re General Realty & Utilities Corp., Del.Ch., 52 A.2d 6, 14–15 (1947). However, to the extent it excludes other generally accepted techniques used in the financial community and the courts, it is now clearly outmoded. It is time we recognize this in appraisal and other stock valuation proceedings and bring our law current on the subject.

While the Chancellor rejected plaintiff's discounted cash flow method of valuing UOP's stock, as not corresponding with "either logic or the existing law" (426 A.2d at 1360), it is significant that this was essentially the focus, i.e., earnings potential of UOP, of Messrs. Arledge and Chitiea in their evaluation of the merger. Accordingly, the standard "Delaware block" or weighted average method of valuation, formerly employed in appraisal and other stock valuation cases, shall no longer exclusively control such proceedings. We believe that a more liberal approach must include proof of value by any techniques or methods which are generally considered acceptable in the financial community and otherwise admissible in court, subject only to our interpretation of 8 Del.C. § 262(h), infra. See also D.R.E. 702–05. This will obviate the very structure and mechanistic procedure that has heretofore governed such matters. . . .

Fair price obviously requires consideration of all relevant factors involving the value of a company. This has long been the law of Delaware as stated in *Tri-Continental Corp.*, 74 A.2d at 72:

> The basic concept of value under the appraisal statute is that the stockholder is entitled to be paid for that which has been taken from him, viz., his proportionate interest in a going concern. By value of the stockholder's proportionate interest in the corporate enterprise is meant the true or intrinsic value of his stock which has been taken by the merger. In determining what figure represents this true or intrinsic value, the appraiser and the courts must take into consideration all factors and elements which reasonably might enter into the fixing of value. Thus, market value, asset value, dividends, earning prospects, the nature of the enterprise and any other facts which were known or which could be ascertained as of the date of merger and which throw any light on *future prospects* of the merged corporation are not only pertinent to an inquiry as to the value of the dissenting stockholders' interest, but *must be considered* by the agency fixing the value. (Emphasis added.)

This is not only in accord with the realities of present day affairs, but it is thoroughly consonant with the purpose and intent of our statutory law. Under 8 Del.C. § 262(h), the Court of Chancery:

> shall appraise the shares, determining their *fair* value exclusive of any element of value arising from the accomplishment or expectation of

the merger, together with a fair rate of interest, if any, to be paid upon the amount determined to be the *fair* value. In determining such *fair* value, the Court shall take into account *all relevant factors* . . . (Emphasis added)

. . .

It is significant that section 262 now mandates the determination of "fair" value based upon "all relevant factors". Only the speculative elements of value that may arise from the "accomplishment or expectation" of the merger are excluded. We take this to be a very narrow exception to the appraisal process, designed to eliminate use of *pro forma* data and projections of a speculative variety relating to the completion of a merger. But elements of future value, including the nature of the enterprise, which are known or susceptible of proof as of the date of the merger and not the product of speculation, may be considered. When the trial court deems it appropriate, fair value also includes any damages, resulting from the taking, which the stockholders sustain as a class. If that was not the case, then the obligation to consider "all relevant factors" in the valuation process would be eroded. We are supported in this view not only by *Tri-Continental Corp.*, 74 A.2d at 72, but also by the evolutionary amendents to section 262.

Prior to an amendment in 1976, the earlier relevant provision of section 262 stated:

(f) The appraiser shall determine the value of the stock of the stockholders . . . The Court shall by its decree determine the value of the stock of the stockholders entitled to payment therefor . . .

The first references to "fair" value occurred in a 1976 amendment to section 262(f), which povided:

(f) . . . the Court shall appraise the shares, determining their fair value exclusively of any element of value arising from the accomplishment or expectation of the merger. . . .

It was not until the 1981 amendment to section 262 that the reference to "fair value" was repeatedly emphasized and the statutory mandate that the Court "take into account all relevant factors" appeared [section 262(h)]. Clearly, there is a legislative intent to fully compensate shareholders for whatever their loss may be, subject only to the narrow limitation that one can not take speculative effects of the merger into account.

Although the Chancellor received the plaintiff's evidence, his opinion indicates that the use of it was precluded because of past Delaware practice. While we do not suggest a monetary result one way or the other, we do think the plaintiff's evidence should be part of the factual mix and weighed as such. Until the $21 price is measured on remand by the valuation standards mandated by Delaware law, there can be no finding at the present stage of these proceedings that the price is fair. Given the lack of any candid disclosure of the material facts surrounding establishment of the $21 price, the majority of the minority vote, approving the merger, is meaningless.

The plaintiff has not sought an appraisal, but rescissory damages of the type contemplated by Lynch v. Vickers Energy Corp., Del.Supr., 429 A.2d

497, 505–06 (1981) (*Lynch II*). In view of the approach to valuation that we announce today, we see no basis in our law for *Lynch II*'s exclusive monetary formula for relief. On remand the plaintiff will be permitted to test the fairness of the $21 price by the standards we herein establish, in conformity with the principle applicable to an appraisal—that fair value be determined by taking "into account all relevant factors" [see 8 Del.C. § 262(h), supra]. In our view this includes the elements of rescissory damages if the Chancellor considers them susceptible of proof and a remedy appropriate to all the issues of fairness before him. To the extent that *Lynch II*, 429 A.2d at 505–06, purports to limit the Chancellor's discretion to a single remedial formula for monetary damages in a cash-out merger, it is overruled.

While a plaintiff's monetary remedy ordinarily should be confined to the more liberalized appraisal proceeding herein established, we do not intend any limitation on the historic powers of the Chancellor to grant such other relief as the facts of a particular case may dictate. The appraisal remedy we approve may not be adequate in certain cases, particularly where fraud, misrepresentation, self-dealing, deliberate waste of corporate assets, or gross and palpable overreaching are involved. Cole v. National Cash Credit Association, Del.Ch., 156 A. 183, 187 (1931). Under such circumstances, the Chancellor's powers are complete to fashion any form of equitable and monetary relief as may be appropriate, including rescissory damages. Since it is apparent that this long completed transaction is too involved to undo, and in view of the Chancellor's discretion, the award, if any, should be in the form of monetary damages based upon entire fairness standards, i.e., fair dealing and fair price.

Obviously, there are other litigants, like the plaintiff, who abjured an appraisal and whose rights to challenge the element of fair value must be preserved. Accordingly, the quasi-appraisal remedy we grant the plaintiff here will apply only to: (1) this case; (2) any case now pending on appeal to this Court; (3) any case now pending in the Court of Chancery which has not yet been appealed but which may be eligible for direct appeal to this Court; (4) any case challenging a cash-out merger, the effective date of which is on or before February 1, 1983; and (5) any proposed merger to be presented at a shareholders' meeting, the notification of which is mailed to the stockholders on or before February 23, 1983. Thereafter, the provisions of 8 Del.C. § 262, as herein construed, respecting the scope of an appraisal and the means for perfecting the same, shall govern the financial remedy available to minority shareholders in a cash-out merger. Thus, we return to the well established principles of Stauffer v. Standard Brands, Inc., Del.Supr., 187 A.2d 78 (1962) and David J. Greene & Co. v. Schenley Industries, Inc., Del.Ch., 281 A.2d 30 (1971), mandating a stockholder's recourse to the basic remedy of an appraisal.

III.

Finally, we address the matter of business purpose. The defendants contend that the purpose of this merger was not a proper subject of inquiry by the trial court. The plaintiff says that no valid purpose existed—the entire transaction was a mere subterfuge designed to eliminate the minority.

The Chancellor ruled otherwise, but in so doing he clearly circumscribed the thrust and effect of *Singer*. Weinberger v. UOP, 426 A.2d at 1342–43, 1348–50. This has led to the thoroughly sound observation that the business purpose test "may be . . . virtually interpreted out of existence, as it was in *Weinberger*".[9]

The requirement of a business purpose is new to our law of mergers and was a departure from prior case law. See Stauffer v. Standard Brands, Inc., supra; David J. Greene & Co. v. Schenley Industries, Inc., supra.

In view of the fairness test which has long been applicable to parent-subsidiary mergers, Sterling v. Mayflower Hotel Corp., Del.Supr., 93 A.2d 107, 109–10 (1952), the expanded appraisal remedy now available to shareholders, and the broad discretion of the Chancellor to fashion such relief as the facts of a given case may dictate, we do not believe that any additional meaningful protection is afforded minority shareholders by the business purpose requirement of the triology of *Singer, Tanzer*,[10] *Najjar*,[11] and their progeny. Accordingly, such requirement shall no longer be of any force or effect.

The judgment of the Court of Chancery, finding both the circumstances of the merger and the price paid the minority shareholders to be fair, is reversed. The matter is remanded for further proceedings consistent herewith. Upon remand the plaintiff's post-trial motion to enlarge the class should be granted.

. . .

Reversed and remanded.

9. Weiss, The Law of Take Out Mergers: A Historical Perspective, 56 N.Y. U.L.Rev. 624, 671, n. 300 (1981).

10. Tanzer v. International General Industries, Inc., Del.Supr., 379 A.2d 1121, 1124–25 (1977).

11. Roland International Corp. v. Najjar, Del.Supr., 407 A.2d 1032, 1036 (1979).

†